TO MAINTAIN AND IMPROVE
THE HISTORY OF THE LOWER AVON NAVIGATION TRUST

TO MAINTAIN AND IMPROVE
THE HISTORY OF THE LOWER AVON NAVIGATION TRUST

D.H. Burlingham

The Memorandum of Association for the Lower Avon Navigation Trust Limited states, *inter alia*: The name of the company (hereinafter called the 'Trust') is The Lower Avon Navigation Trust Limited. The objects for which the trust is established are: To maintain and improve the navigation of the river Avon between the junction thereof with the river Severn at Tewkesbury in the County of Gloucester, and the Town of Evesham in the County of Worcester...

TEMPUS

First published 2000

PUBLISHED IN THE UNITED KINGDOM BY:

Tempus Publishing Ltd
The Mill, Brimscombe Port
Stroud, Gloucestershire GL5 2QG

PUBLISHED IN THE UNITED STATES OF AMERICA BY:

Arcadia Publishing Inc.
A division of Tempus Publishing Inc.
2 Cumberland Street
Charleston, SC 29401
(Tel: 1-888-313-2665)

Tempus books are available in France, Germany and Belgium
from the following addresses:

Tempus Publishing Group	Tempus Publishing Group	Tempus Publishing Group
21 Avenue de la République	Gustav-Adolf-Straße 3	Place de L'Alma 4/5
37300 Joué-lès-Tours	99084 Erfurt	1200 Brussels
FRANCE	GERMANY	BELGIUM

British Library Cataloguing in Publication Data.
A catalogue record for this book is available from the British Library.

ISBN 0 7524 1756 8

Typesetting and origination by Tempus Publishing.
PRINTED AND BOUND IN GREAT BRITAIN.

Contents

Acknowledgements

It would not have been possible to write and illustrate this book without the support of many people, to whom I am most grateful.

Lord Walker has written a succinct foreword in which he recalls his acquaintance with the Trust as a busy Minister of State almost thirty years ago.

Mrs D.A. Hilton has most kindly allowed the use of a picture from her late husband's book *Tewkesbury and the Vale of Gloucester in Old Photographs*.

Douglas Barwell's diaries of the restoration (1950-1962), copies of which he gave to his close associates including me, have provided a core material source for events during that period.

In particular Lord Sandys, David Cottrell, Pat Edwards, David Gittins, Trevor Gray, Dennis Hall, Leslie Haines, Ray Harrison, Bill Holyoak and Dudley Mathews have between them revived old memories, produced pictures and told me things I did not know. Nicholas Barwell allowed access to a superb photographic record and to various papers. The Almonry Museum Evesham, Tewkesbury Town Council, Worcestershire County Record Office and Daniel Burlingham have been most helpful with pictures and diagrams. My wife and Sally Issler have pointed me in appropriate directions at times of uncertainty. Essentially Ann Stephens has most skilfully translated my often illegible pencilled manuscript into a word processed draft and with great patience accepted innumerable changes.

The hundreds of people who helped to restore the Lower Avon Navigation, and who later helped, and still do help, to run it have made this history possible. Put another way, they are themselves the history.

DHB June 2000

The author acknowledges that any opinions expressed in this narrative are his, and do not necessarily reflect those of others.

Foreword

By the Rt Hon. The Lord Walker of Worcester MBE PC

I am delighted that David Burlingham has put pen to paper and written this excellent history of The Lower Avon Navigation Trust (LANT) which is particularly appropriate at the fiftieth anniversary of LANT. It is marvellous that a group of individuals took on the enormous task of restoring the navigation of the Lower River Avon between 1950 and 1962 and ensured that it has been able to be available for navigation in the years since.

I well remember my pleasure during the period I was the first ever Secretary of State for the Environment when I was asked to formally open the new 'A' frame lock-keeper's house at Evesham, now nearly thirty years ago.

We are very lucky in England to have many marvellous rivers. If we are not constantly vigilant these rivers, instead of being places of beauty providing wonderful relaxation and recreation for people, will become areas that are not available for navigation and purely areas of pollution.

I hope this book will be read not just by those of us in Worcestershire who benefit from what has taken place, but by others throughout the country who can follow the splendid example that David Burlingham and his colleagues set and do similar work to the benefit of the nation's environment.

10 May 2000

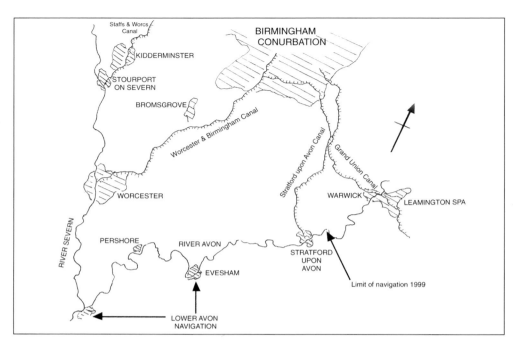

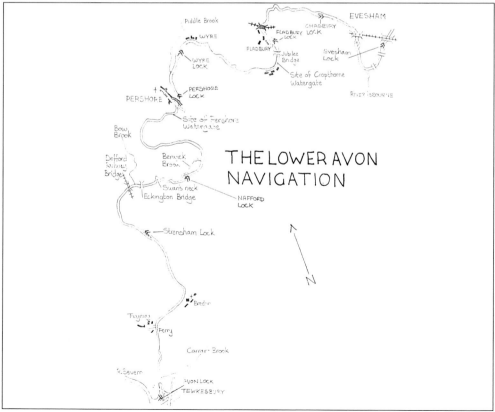

Part I Background
1 The beginning

In the middle and late 1940s three apparently unrelated events occurred, which when connected with another activity begun in the late 1930s, coalesced into what eventually became The Lower Avon Navigation Trust: a book was published in 1944; a while later a London-based author and literary agent read a review of the book and bought a copy; a Midlands industrialist had a boat holiday and a River Board was improving a river. All very disparate happenings.

But to see how these events relate and come together, it is necessary to put the whole into a geographical and historical context.

There are four rivers Avon in England alone; the one with which we are concerned is commonly known as the Warwickshire Avon, or Shakespeare's Avon, although the part which concerns this narrative flows mainly through Worcestershire. The river has its source in the village of Naseby in Northamptonshire. It flows by Welford in Northamptonshire, (not to be confused with Welford-on-Avon), Stanford-on-Avon, Rugby, below the walls of Warwick Castle, Stratford-upon-Avon, Welford-on-Avon, Bidford-on-Avon; and now the part that concerns this story: Evesham, Pershore and Tewkesbury where it joins the river Severn, – a total length of roughly 110 miles.

Of passing interest is that the decisive battles of the three English civil wars were fought on the banks of the river. In 1269 the outcome of the 'Baron's War' was decided at Evesham when the army of Prince Edward, later to become Edward I, defeated and killed Simon De Montfort, founder of the Parliamentary system. At Tewkesbury the Lancastrian cause was ended by Edward IV in 1471, and at Naseby the Royalists were defeated by Oliver Cromwell in 1645.

In the Avon valley three great Benedictine monastic institutions and their abbeys were built, at Evesham, Pershore and Tewkesbury. The institutions were all destroyed by Henry VIII. The Abbey at Tewkesbury survives intact: of that at Pershore only the choir and tower remain; Evesham Abbey, the largest of the three, was destroyed in 1539, and only its separate Bell Tower remains.

The development of the river over the centuries follows in its early stages that of many similar rivers in England. As pre-Saxon settlements were established and grew along its banks, each largely self-sufficient in producing the staple necessities of food and timber, it became necessary to find a source of power to produce the increasing amount of flour needed to feed an expanding population. Low lying riparian settlements were not well situated for wind power, and the Avon is not naturally fast flowing. It became necessary to raise water levels artificially in places to provide a difference in levels, thereby creating a power source to drive water wheels. The early impoundment dams were probably little more than rows of wooden stakes driven into the river bed, interwoven with wattle and infilled with clay – enough to hold back the water. A mill building, probably consisting of a rough timber frame, walls filled with wattle and daub, and a crude reed thatch roof, would house the primitive machinery used to grind the corn, probably driven by an undershot mill wheel. The building would keep the grain and flour sheltered from the elements. These fragile structures were doubtless destroyed by most floods, and so gradually the millers would have developed more durable dams and buildings. The basic structures of many of the existing weirs on the Lower Avon remain unchanged to this day: wooden stakes (many of which may have been in situ for hundreds of years and are as sound as the day they were driven) infilled and packed with impermeable clay, stone faced top and bottom and capped with stones set on edge. More recently, the weir crests (tops) and toes (bottoms) have been strengthened with steel piles and the glacis (slope) capped with steel-reinforced concrete.

By the time of the Doomsday Survey in 1085, at least five mills at Pershore, Wyre, Fladbury, Chadbury and Evesham were of sufficient importance to record; there may well have been others.

The importance of the millers' rights to their difference in water levels, or head of water, were and still are of great importance. The millers were entirely dependent on this source of power for their living, and the local population were in turn dependent on the miller for their bread. Disruption, whether by flood or other means, was a very serious matter. Even fifty years ago, when only two mills on the Lower Avon actually used water power, not only those two mill owners, but also those who had converted mills into houses were very possessive of their rights to a head of water.

As the decades and centuries rolled by, the river continued to flow, draining its large catchment area: eroding banks when in spate after heavy rainfall, carrying and depositing silt; in times of drought being little more in places than a muddy stream. As villages and towns in the valley gradually developed and local populations grew, a need arose to trade agricultural produce, lime, iron, stone and other commodities. This trade was severely restricted by the state of such roads as then existed – mainly muddy, if well-used, unsurfaced tracks, which allowed loads no greater than a pack horse could carry. Undoubtedly some goods would have been moved on the river by primitive craft, but this method of transport would have been restricted by the relatively short distance between the millers' dams. As early as the reign of Henry IV (1367-1413), the Earl of Warwick was 'mynded to have made a passage for boattes from Tewkesbury to Warwick for transportyng of merchantdise for the advantage of Warwick.' The Duke of Clarence (1449-1478) showed a like interest, but no action followed.

To advance further it would be necessary to overcome the barrier of the millers' dams.

The early Navigation
In 1633 William Sandys, son of Sir William Sandys of Brimpsfield and Miserden, Gloucestershire, together with his younger brother, obtained from the Bishop of Worcester a lease of the manor of Fladbury near Pershore, which they held until the Civil War. There is no mention of Sandys in Fladbury parish records, so it is unlikely that he lived there. He was a man of position and influence, a Justice of the Peace and Member of Parliament for the Borough of Evesham both before and after the Civil War. He went

up to Oxford, to Gloucester Hall, later to be called Worcester College, in 1623. The principal of Gloucester Hall, Dr John Hawley, was one of the Commissioners appointed under the Thames Act of 1623-1624 to oversee the building of navigation works on the Upper Thames between Oxford and Buscot.

We can surmise that on the Thames some pound locks and watergates were being built in order to improve the depths of water for larger sized boats in the upper reaches. It is almost certain that Sandys' interest in, and knowledge of, civil engineering works developed at that time.

Pound locks, so called because they enabled boats to move from one river level or pound to another (a pound is a reach or stretch of water between locks or dams), were chambers constructed of brick or stone, usually on timber foundations, or in some instances with turf sides, and of sufficient size to accommodate a moderately sized boat. At each end of the chamber was an entrance/exit of watertight gates containing sluices (or paddles in waterway parlance) for the admission or release of water. To pass from a lower water level to a higher, the boat entered the lock chamber, closed the lower lock gates and paddles, then opened the upper paddles to admit water into the lock chamber. When the water level inside the lock chamber reached the upper level outside, the upper lock gates could be opened and the boat moved to the upper level of water. To pass in the opposite direction the procedure is reversed. This operation caused minimum disturbance to water levels, using only one chamber full of water, and it was therefore acceptable to the millers.

A watergate was a single watertight gate with paddles, in a dam which might comprise more large sluices and a weir. To pass through dam and watergate, water levels had to be equal on both sides. The gate was opened, the boat passed through, moored, and the gate, gate paddles and all other sluices in the dam were closed. The upstream water thus impounded rose until there was sufficient depth for the boat to proceed. Travelling downstream, the gate, gate paddles and sluices were first closed, and the water level raised before the boat could travel to the upper side of the watergate. The gate paddles and sluices could then be opened, the resulting fall in water level allowing the gate to be opened and the boat to proceed. This whole operation was very cumbersome in use: the gate itself required winches on the bank both to open and close it. In theory one person could operate it – in practice at least three people were needed. Floating debris in the river blocked the main sluices and needed constant clearance. The operation affected the water levels on the upper side of the structure. Where a mill or a ford was situated upstream, both could be made temporarily unusable – a great conflict of interest between miller and ford users on the one part and boat users on the other. In times of drought the upper level could take very many hours and even days to fill to a usable depth.

These navigation works interested Sandys, who saw enormous potential for creating a commercial enterprise by improving river navigations elsewhere.

The lease of the manor of Fladbury in 1633 gave Sandys riparian access to the river and weir at Fladbury. He must have started work on the river soon after obtaining this access, but soon discovered that there was likely to be considerable opposition from landowners and millers to his overall scheme; he also realised that he would be unable to fund the works from his own resources. Sandys therefore petitioned Charles I and in 1635 obtained an Order in Council which appointed thirty Commissioners and gave him the legal right

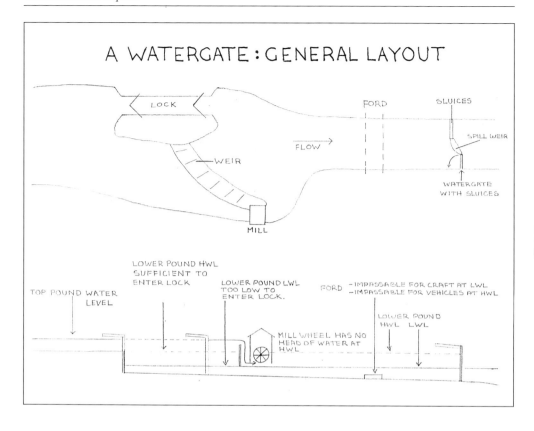

A WATERGATE: GENERAL LAYOUT

to purchase the necessary lands, the size of which was defined, for the construction of locks, sluices and weirs for the purpose of making 'the river of Avon…Passable for Boates of reasonable Burthen from Severn where that River falls in nere Teuxbury…unto or neare the citty of Coventry…'. While this Order in Council helped, opposition continued and further recourse to the King was necessary the following year.

There are differing views as to how long it took to complete the construction of what is believed to be fourteen pound locks, two watergates and other navigation works between Tewkesbury and Stratford. Some authorities, such as Treadway Nash's *Worcestershire*, published in 1781 a century later (see Appendix A) say it was done by 1639. This would be a prodigious engineering feat even in current times, given the availability of the resources required in the form of skilled and unskilled labour, timber and stone which would have to be transported to sites, and cash to pay for the work. Other authorities give 1666 as a completion date, which seems more realistic. (See Appendix B.) Between these dates came the Civil War, following which Sandys was debarred from Parliament and made to give up his river interests to a prominent anti-royalist judge, William Say. Bridges at Evesham and Pershore were destroyed during hostilities, blocking the river and leading to a cessation of river traffic and consequent neglect of locks. Repairs were subsequently made by Say, restoring the Navigation between Tewkesbury and Evesham. Whichever completion date is accepted, the Avon was the first river in England

Evesham Bridge c.1800, viewed from upstream with masted vessel.

to be made navigable by means of pound locks.

Following the Restoration of the Monarchy, the repaired navigation works and rights were bought by Lord Windsor, one of the original Commissioners appointed in 1636. Lord Windsor involved others, giving or selling to them various proportions or complete parts of the whole undertaking. Thus the division of the Lower (Tewkesbury-Evesham) and Upper (Evesham-Stratford) Avon Navigations gradually came about, finally occurring in 1717.

No detailed descriptive account survives of the type of craft used for cargo carrying on the river. They would have varied in size. Contemporary illustrations show what appear to be wide beam, flat-bottomed craft 30-40ft long by about 14ft wide, with a carrying capacity of about 30 tons. A mast with a square sail is shown; the mast would have to be lowered to pass beneath bridges. These craft were normally bow-hauled by gangs of men, the sail being used to assist only when conditions allowed. Severn trows were of similar build, but larger.

The later Navigations
The subsequent history of the two Navigations, Lower and Upper, is both complex and long. It has been well recorded by others and makes fascinating study.

To summarise the vast amount of detail, it must suffice for this account to say that both Navigations enjoyed varying periods of prosperity and decline, and to pick out only the principal events and changes. Although the two Navigations were separate entities, the prosperity of one directly affected that of the other. Such was the confusion over charges made for transport of goods on the river, that a regulatory Act of Parliament was passed in 1751. This not only set out detailed charges for a wide range of goods, it also required the Navigation proprietors to spend toll income on maintenance of locks and associated works and made the Avon a 'Free River', enabling anyone to use it on payment of the appropriate charges, removing the proprietors' previously held monopoly for the carriage of goods. Shortly after this time the Windsor interests in the Lower Avon were bought by a London lawyer, George Perrott. The state of the Lower Navigation was then very poor, requiring Perrott to spend over £4,000 on restoration – a very substantial sum – suggesting that the commercial potential of the Navigation was large. George Perrott died in 1776 and was succeeded by his nephew – also named George Perrott.

We now come to the period known as the dawn of Britain's Industrial Revolution. Steam power was driving the nation's factories. Improved and more transport was needed to bring raw materials to factories and to distribute finished articles. The only alternative to the very poor roads of the period was water, and that was confined to navigable rivers, such as the Avon. Artificial waterways – canals – would expand transport routes. An era of canal building began.

One of the canals promoted was the Stratford-upon-Avon Canal, in which the younger Perrott had a interest, and which he saw would be in direct competition for some of the Avon traffic. He therefore persuaded his fellow promoters to include in the 1793 Enabling Act for the canal a requirement for the canal proprietors to pay to the Lower Avon proprietors an annuity of £400 per annum – a large sum at that time and one which would equal only a part of the overall toll income of the Lower Avon. This annuity is still paid today and will feature later in this story.

Another canal linking the Severn at Worcester to the great Birmingham conurbation was constructed. The Stratford-upon-Avon canal joined it at Kings Norton, near Birmingham.

While these new waterways took quite substantial traffic from the river, there still remained sufficient to provide a viable income to the proprietors of both Upper and Lower Navigations.

While not directly concerned with this story, it can be noted that Perrott House in Bridge Street, Pershore, a Grade I Georgian town house (destroyed by fire in 1998 and currently being rebuilt) was built by the elder George Perrott who lived in it from 1755 until his death. The younger George Perrott built Craycombe House near Fladbury – a Grade II Georgian country mansion. The cost of both houses was probably met, at least in part, by the profits of the Lower Avon Navigation.

The new canals in the Midlands were being built to a general standard design to accommodate craft 70ft long by just under 7ft beam. This immediately presented a problem to both Avon Navigations. On the Upper Navigation all the locks were too short, as were some on the Lower Navigation. Until this could be changed, through traffic with the canal system was not possible.

The condition of the Upper Avon in the early part of the nineteenth century was very poor, and there was the added problem of short locks. Its then owner, William James, closed the river for some months in 1822 and spent some £6,000 on its refurbishment, which did not include lengthening locks on every site. Partly because of poor receipts from river tolls, James was unable to repay loans and became bankrupt. The Upper Avon Navigation was then bought by a syndicate of seven people, who carried out further works, resulting in a temporary improvement in fortune.

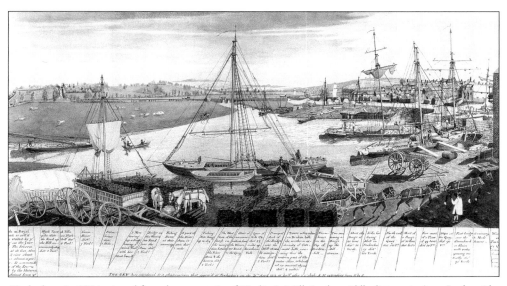

Tewkesbury in 1804, viewed from the present site of Healing's Mill. In the middle distance is Avon Lock, with masted vessel, and beyond the lock King John's Bridge. In the right background is Bredon Hill.

In 1826 a horse tramway from Stratford-upon-Avon to Moreton-in-Marsh was completed, bringing a small amount of badly needed trade to the river.

The Perrott fortunes fell into decline, and the ownership of the Lower Avon Navigation passed to Perrott Trustees in 1835, while the operating rights on the lower river were sold.

The Upper Avon syndicate leased their part of the river to the Stratford Canal Company for five years in 1842. The 1850s saw the first railways in the area. The Upper Avon by then had ceased to be commercially viable; the owners stopped taking tolls, leaving river users to fend for themselves. Also at this time the Stratford Canal was bought by the Oxford, Worcester and Wolverhampton Railway, which employed a manager, John Broughton. Could the railway company be persuaded to buy the Upper Avon Navigation as well, thereby extending the canal's trading? Following discussions with Broughton, he – not the railway company – bought the Upper Avon Navigation. There is much confusion as to how the deal was actually done. It is generally accepted that Broughton acted as nominee of the railway company, which in due course became part of the Great Western Railway. The railway company continued to take tolls for a while, minute as they were, but did no maintenance work on the river. Only one boat now operated to Stratford Mills, and it was only part loaded because of shoals. In due course the Great Western Railway opened a branch line to Stratford, and another rival railway company did the same. When this happened in 1875, the Great Western Railway stopped taking tolls and abandoned the river to its fate.

The river users took the Great Western Railway to court in 1877, but lost their case on a technicality. They were advised that an appeal would succeed, but they had neither the funds nor the enthusiasm to fight.

An unsuccessful attempt to revive the moribund Upper Avon Navigation was made in

Defford Railway Bridge. Engineer's impression dated 1839, just before the bridge was built. Artistic license has been used to show Eckington Bridge and the steepness of Bredon Hill.

1895. The Mayor of Evesham called a meeting of local authorities and other interested parties. An elaborate scheme of funding was devised and recommended, but some of the respective constituent authorities would not accept it. The rejection of the scheme was a shock to its promoters and to many local people.

In 1899 a River Avon Improvement Association was formed which did much work in lobbying local authorities and in informing local opinion. In 1905 the Association published a forty-eight page booklet: *The River Avon. Why its navigation should be restored and how it may be done*. Their efforts came to nothing.

In 1912 a further attempt was made by local people to promote an Avon Conservancy for the whole river. Another booklet was published: *Avon Navigation, Suggested Scheme for the Restoration of the River*. This scheme also failed to gain the necessary support. Two years later the First World War began, and attention was diverted elsewhere.

One last attempt was made in 1919-20. A very ambitious scheme was put before central government, which had set up a committee on inland waterways, but it also failed. So the Upper Avon remained in its decayed state, its ruined locks gradually disappearing beneath mud, reeds and trees; some can still be found today. The Navigation itself remained derelict until rescue commenced in 1968. But that is another story...

The late nineteenth and early twentieth centuries
Meanwhile, limited trade continued on the Lower Avon. Mills at Evesham, Pershore and Tewkesbury received regular deliveries of grain and there were occasional loads of other goods, including iron and lime. In spite of the introduction of a steam powered barge, *The Bee,* in 1862, toll paying traffic gradually declined.

A new type of traffic began to develop – pleasure steamers. Railways could now bring many hundreds of day trippers from towns and cities to the riverside towns where river

PLEASURE GARDENS. EVESHAM

Steamers at Evesham c.1900, winter.

journeys could be enjoyed. By the turn of the century passenger steamers were making regular trips from Evesham to Tewkesbury. Under the 1751 Act they did not have to pay tolls, although most steamer operators had informal agreements to contribute towards the upkeep of the Navigation. Owners of private launches, rowing boats and punts were also encouraged to make modest contributions. But this income did not match the repair costs, and gradually the condition of locks, sluices and weirs deteriorated.

By 1921, the beneficiaries of the Perrott Trust had received no income for some years, and in 1923 they sold their Lower Avon interests to Perrott Stimson and Walter Fisher, who founded the Lower Avon Navigation Company Limited. The assets of this company comprised the navigation rights, the locks, other (unspecified) navigation works and properties and the £400 annuity already described. For the most part weirs on the river, and their upkeep, were the responsibility of the respective millers. The new company tried hard to do what repairs it could with its limited income, but it was fighting a losing battle.

To try to improve matters in 1932, the company took the bold step of promoting a private Bill in Parliament which would, *inter alia*, give the proprietors of the Lower Avon powers to increase tolls (set by the 1751 Act and regulated by subsequent Canal Acts) and to charge tolls on all pleasure traffic. There was strong local opposition, because provision in the Bill would allow Stimson and Fisher to recoup their legal costs before applying any increased toll income towards very badly needed essential maintenance and repairs. The Bill failed and the unsatisfactory status quo remained. All the locks were operable with varying degrees of difficulty when the Second World War began in 1939. (See Appendix C.)

During the war there was virtually no activity on the river. *Pisgah,* the 30 ton grain barge, continued to run from Avonmouth, Sharpness or Gloucester to Partridge's mill at Pershore, as she had done since 1918. *Pisgah's* crew did minimal maintenance to keep the four locks and one watergate usable; upstream from Pershore four locks and one watergate fell into decay and by the end of the war in 1945 were completely derelict and unusable.

Chadbury Lock c.1890. Note the deteriorating wall to the left.

In 1946 Stimson and Fisher sold the Lower Avon Navigation Company Limited to John Whitehouse, an Evesham Borough Alderman and member of Worcestershire County Council. The company owned the navigation rights, four locks and one watergate which were just functional, two locks and one watergate which were derelict, some properties, and the £400 annuity, which at that time represented the size of income on which a man and wife could live very moderately. Some years later it became apparent that Whitehouse attempted to sell the Navigation twice; it became clear that he had little concern for it. Minimal effort was made to collect the very small toll income and no proper accounts were kept; it was obvious that his only interest was the receipt of the annuity.

To put into context what then followed on the Lower Avon, the state of the country as a whole, and of the Vale of Evesham in particular, should be understood.

For six years since 1939, Britain had been fighting for existence. Although it emerged victorious, the country was exhausted. The fit and able population had been drafted into the armed services or into essential war work in mines, factories and farms. Food and raw materials of all kinds were severely rationed. By 1945 the infrastructure of the country: railways, roads, the remaining canals and navigable rivers, railway wagons, road vehicles, barges, electricity, gas and water supply systems, was worn out. The nation was virtually bankrupt, its resources were spent and there were no funds available to buy even essential imports. The population as a whole, although healthy, was undernourished and weary – physically and mentally: it had had enough.

And now attention had to be given to rebuilding the country, its infrastructure and its institutions; it was a matter of export or die. From producing armaments and the necessities for waging war, production had to be switched – and quickly – to making goods which could be sold in exchange for funds with which vital raw materials from overseas could be purchased. Tough wartime conditions became even worse in some cases. It was more of same!

After 1945 armed service personnel were gradually demobilised. Supplies of materials

Fladbury Lock, 1900. Note the Lower Avon type paddle gear and the rake of the gates.

and food continued to be rationed. Materials priorities were: first to make goods for export, then for the rebuilding of the vital parts of the nation's infrastructure, repairing war damaged houses and factories and for building new houses for the many thousands of returning servicemen. Official Permits had to be obtained before most materials could be purchased or used. After many months or even years on waiting lists, some new civilian goods could be purchased: machine tools for factories, commercial vehicles, utility clothing (still rationed), utility furniture, simple household items, even motor cars. High class, luxury goods were strictly for export only.

In the Vale of Evesham during the war and immediately afterwards, every available piece of land grew food crops or was used for airfields or military camps. At one time during the war the local population was outnumbered by American service personnel. On the land horse power was slowly changing to tractor power. What the rather insular population of the Vale did not know about growing food crops and other like pursuits was not worth knowing, and furthermore they needed no interference from 'Brummies' and other similar ignorant townspeople. So, as far as the Avon Navigation was concerned, there were other far more important things to be done in the Vale. And for the very few people who knew anything about it, the failed attempts of 1932, 1920, 1912, 1905 and 1895 offered no encouragement.

However, during the 1940s, the war and immediate post-war years, civilisation, recreation and culture did continue, albeit in muted form; it became in a sense even more precious because so much of it was destroyed or made difficult by the war and its aftermath. Music was composed and performed; some people did take holidays and take part in sporting activities; pictures were painted and exhibited; books were written and published; which leads to a more full account of the time when the four apparently unrelated events occurred, all of which would influence the future of the navigation of the Lower Avon: a book published, a review of the book read, a river holiday and a River Board.

Fladbury Lock, 1950. An interesting comparison with the picture on the previous page.

Fladbury Lock, 1950.

Part II Restoration
2 A dream into reality

A book…a review…a river holiday…a River Board. How did these separate events connect?

Narrow Boat, written in 1940, first published in 1944 and through several editions never out of print since, was a graphic description of a lengthy canal journey made on a converted narrow boat in 1939. It describes very vividly not only the canals, how they were made and how they were worked, but also the boat people who worked the canals, how they lived and the skills they developed. The author, L.T.C. Rolt, was a mechanical engineer turned philosopher, and an enthusiast for the protection of the artefacts, skills, and landscapes of the countryside – including canals. He became the writer of very readable books on subjects as diverse as railways, biographies of engineers, waterways, engineering history and topography.

A review of the book was read by a London-based author and literary agent, Robert Aickman, who had also developed what he described as a 'mild interest' in canals, although from an entirely different standpoint from that of Rolt. Aickman initially learned about canals 'from the bank', although he later travelled widely on them. He became appalled by their insidious depredation and deliberate neglect by 'Authority.'

The river holiday was taken by a Midlands industrialist Charles Douglas Barwell – known by his second name. His family business was the manufacture of brass and copper tubes. Not only was he a shrewd businessman, he was also a very competent and practical engineer. By 1949 a modest ration of petrol was available for recreational purposes, and Barwell had a sufficient allowance for his petrol-engined cruiser *North Star* to enable him to take a family holiday afloat. With his wife and baby son he left his mooring at the Severn Motor Yacht Club on the River Severn – then a very busy commercial waterway – and turned into the Avon. At Avon Lock, Tewkesbury he locked up onto the Avon, no doubt helping the lock-keeper there, Arch Collins, to work the winches that were necessary to force open the leaking lock gates. Strensham Lock was just usable, the lock gates had to be winched open from the bank. At Nafford Lock *North Star* became trapped: the lower lock gates leaked so badly that it was almost impossible to fill the lock; the upper gates were very stiff to move. A visit to the nearby Woollas Hall Farm enabled Barwell to obtain a supply of straw with which to make temporary plugs to the gaping holes in the gates. *North Star* eventually proceeded to Pershore, with Barwell's temper and curiosity both aroused. Why was the Navigation in such a shocking state? Who better to ask than the owners of *Pisgah*, the Partridge brothers of Pershore Mill. Barwell learned the background to the decrepit state of the river; the lock installations kept working by constant 'bodging' by *Pisgah's* crew, and the Partridge brothers wondering how long before a major breakdown at one of the locks would halt their use of water transport. Barwell finished his eventful holiday by returning to the Severn on *North Star*.

The Severn River Board's Lower Avon Improvement Scheme was first considered in the 1920s by its predecessor bodies, the Three Counties Land Drainage Authority and later the River Severn Catchment Board. Its main object was to enhance land drainage in the Avon valley by obtaining greater flows in the river after high rainfall, and thereby reducing the effects of flooding. Starting in the mid-1930s with the installation of a radial sluice gate at Abbey Mill, Tewkesbury, then shortly afterwards a new sluice at Stanchard Pit, Tewkesbury, the scheme also included river channel excavation to provide an improved channel capacity. The scheme continued upstream – a few miles each year – to Pershore, and by the early 1960s much improved sluice control structures and channel capacity had been provided. In 1950 work was proceeding in the Comberton area. The scheme was funded by Ministry of Agriculture and Fisheries land drainage grants (30%) and by Local Authority precepts (70%). The effect of the scheme on the Navigation was to provide a more than adequate navigation channel while at the same time preserving the existing retention levels in river pounds.

The Severn River Board later became the Severn River Authority, which in turn became part of the Severn Trent Water Authority, then subsequently part of the National Rivers Authority. It is currently part of the Environmental Agency.

As a result of reading the review of *Narrow Boat*, Aickman bought a copy, and many months later he wrote to Rolt suggesting the formation of a Society, 'something like the Friends of Canterbury Cathedral' to do something about the decline of canal systems. The two men met, and cutting short a very long story, they and others founded the Inland Waterways Association – known as IWA – in 1946 with Aickman as chairman. Its objects were the '...use, maintenance and development of the inland waterways of the British Isles...the restoration to good order of every navigable waterway...' Gradually they gathered support from all over the country. By 1948, IWA had grown so much that a midlands branch, based in Birmingham, was formed. As an active campaigning organisation, the midlands branch soon learned about the almost derelict state of the Lower Avon.

With his interest stirred by his holiday struggles, Barwell

> ...wrote to the IWA and became a member. In return I received a communication from Robert Aickman, this eventually leading me to be invited to become a committee member of the IWA's midlands branch.

The branch determined on action to stop further deterioration of the Lower Avon before it became completely lost to navigation. It was clear that the current proprietor, Whitehouse, could and would do nothing, and so it was decided that the IWA midlands branch should itself acquire the Lower Avon Navigation. After much discussion, Barwell agreed

> ....to act as nominee of the IWA and to provide – on legally agreed terms – the necessary finance with which to purchase the entire share capital of the existing but very dormant Lower Avon Navigation Company.

Wyre Lock, 1950. Silted up lock chamber. The remains of the lower lock gate can be seen on the right.

After negotiations with Whitehouse, Barwell purchased the whole share capital of 1000 shares for £1,500. The contract was completed in April 1950. The assets transferred were the navigation rights including, most importantly, the existing navigation water retention levels★, and the freehold of the lock sites and associated works; the annuity was specifically excluded from the purchase.

The locks themselves, four of which were usable with difficulty and three of which were derelict, plus one just usable and one derelict watergate were seventeenth century structures, restored in the eighteenth century and repaired from time to time since. They had been designed and built for the traffic and vessels of their time. Their overall dimensions were already established.

Now the proprietors of a river navigation, the IWA midlands branch formed an Avon

★*Possessing the navigation water retention levels was and is vital for the ability to navigate the river. Inadequate levels would make navigation very difficult if not impossible. The subsequent restoration of the Upper Avon Navigation between Evesham and Stratford-upon-Avon (1965-1974), where the old retention levels had long been destroyed and abandoned – except on the reaches above Evesham, Welford and Stratford Weirs – required the establishment and acceptance of new water retention levels against much initial local opposition.*

Fladbury Lock, 1950. Downstream gates, no balance arms; silted up lock chamber.

Chadbury Lock, 1950. Bottom gates.

sub-committee with Barwell as chairman. Its terms of reference were to deal with all Avon matters and to establish a new organisation to restore the Lower Avon Navigation – probably in the form of a charitable trust.

Restore – for that is what would be necessary – a semi-derelict river navigation: what an undertaking! No one had ever done anything like it before. Where on earth to start? What exactly needed to be done? Who would do it? How was it to be financed? Who would be sufficiently interested and concerned to get involved in such a stupid enterprise anyway?

The beginnings of the Lower Avon Navigation Trust
The whole idea of a restoration project was inadvisable, foolish, mad, – harmless perhaps – but nevertheless most peculiar. Who on earth would want to be associated with it, let alone give it the active support it would need if it was to have any chance at all of success?

It is an understatement to say that the early months of 1950 were busy ones for Barwell. First he had to make a general assessment of the whole Navigation, inspecting lock sites to obtain a good idea of their overall condition. It was not an encouraging inspection. It was necessary also to talk to as many people as possible with detailed knowledge of the river: the Partridge brothers at Pershore Mill, to learn precisely the problems of navigating *Pisgah* on the river; J.L. Sanders, boat builder, at Pensham and L.A. Robinson of Bathhursts, Tewkesbury who operated a hire cruiser fleet produced information about the problems experienced by owners of privately owned craft and of hire craft users. There were meetings and talks with many others mostly living or working in the Avon valley, who could help build up a picture of what had to be done.

Besides the physical hands-on engineering works, the need for which was abundantly clear, there was the absolutely vital need to acquire credibility for this vast enterprise. No such project had ever been attempted before, the river had a record of failed rescue attempts, four on the Upper Avon and one on the Lower; and most of the local population were either completely indifferent or hostile towards it. What could a mere 'Brummie' do about what was essentially a local problem – if it was a problem at all? And there was, as yet, no body corporate with competent officers to guide and operate this madcap scheme, only a committee of 'Brummies' (the IWA midlands branch Avon sub-committee) who made the occasional foray to the river and then retreated to their Birmingham/Black Country fastnesses. 'Brummies', to the inhabitants of the Vale of Evesham, were a strange people from the Black Country, and the Birmingham-Coventry conurbation to the north. True, the midlands and local press had expressed genuine interest in the change of ownership, and in the case of the locally influential *Evesham Journal* and *Four Shires Advertiser* shown very positive support, but that was a very long way indeed from anything actually being done. Credibility can only be earned by sensible deeds and action.

A chance to prove this came all too soon. In March 1950 there was a major failure at Strensham Lock. This time it was beyond a bodged repair. A new pair of lock gates was the only sensible solution, – but from where? Lock gates have to be specially made and

Chadbury Lock, 1950. The bottom gates are silted up, planking and balance arms are missing and the lock chamber is overgrown.

installed by skilled and experienced craftsmen.

The Avon sub-committee authorised Barwell to approach the Docks and Inland Waterways Executive (DIWE), a newly nationalised body and predecessor of British Waterways, to ask for their advice and help. DIWE had a large and well equipped workshop at Diglis, Worcester and a very experienced and skilled staff who were responsible for the maintenance of the locks and weirs★ on the river Severn. After negotiations, they agreed to make and install a new pair of upstream (top) lock gates, a process which would take about two months and would have to be fitted round their other commitments on the very busy river Severn. While these gates were being installed, they would inspect the whole lock and advise on possible replacement of the downstream (bottom) lock gates. The new top gates were fitted in June and the Navigation reopened, after a closure of only three and a half months, proving to anyone concerned that there was a determination to get things done. A new pair of bottom lock gates were fitted in September, and during the summer volunteer working parties had cleared overgrown trees and vegetation round the lock and repaired and rebuilt large sections of brickwork. By October the Navigation had a fully reconditioned working lock.

★*The weirs on the river Severn were designed and constructed during the nineteenth century, impounding the river for navigational purposes only.*

Strensham Lock, 1950. Lower gates. C.D. Barwell points to problems.

Back now to March 1950. The IWA Avon sub-committee decided that the new organisation, when formed, should be called 'The Lower Avon Navigation Trust'. Discussion proceeded with solicitors on the formation of a non-profit making company limited by guarantee and having no share holders, but membership by payment of an annual subscription. Officers and directors, or Council members, as they were called, were to receive no payment. The legal Articles and Memorandum of the Company would include a requirement '...to maintain and improve the Navigation...', and would be in a form acceptable for charitable status. Their general content was later followed as a general legal pattern for the formation of many other similar bodies. A Secretary and Honorary Treasurer, both important officers, were needed for the new company. Local enquiries in Evesham led Barwell to Police Superintendent E.J. Price, about to retire after many years service, and to P.H. Protheroe, manager of the Evesham branch of the National Provincial Bank (now the National Westminster Bank); both these men were very highly regarded in the Vale of Evesham. People to become the first subscribers to the legal Articles, and who would become the first directors or members of the Council, had to be found. With the advice of Price and Protheroe, Barwell approached a representative section of 'the great and the good' of the Avon valley, together with other well-regarded representatives of boating and IWA interests; all with one exception agreed to serve. These first subscribers included the Mayors or Chairman and Clerks of Evesham Borough Council, Evesham Rural District Council,

Strensham Lock, 1950. The start of the first restoration job. Foreman Munn and the DIWE gang are installing the upstream stank before removing the beyond-repair upstream lockgates.

Pershore Rural District Council, Tewkesbury Borough Council, some other members of these authorities and the founder chairman of the IWA. Looking at this list of individuals, any potential supporters could have complete confidence that the new Trust would succeed in its objectives.

The first meeting of the new Lower Avon Navigation Trust took place in July, when it formally succeeded the IWA midlands branch Avon sub-committee as the proprietor of the Lower Avon Navigation.

The Trust had no money in the bank; it owed Barwell £1,500 for the purchase of the Navigation. Its immediate predecessors – the IWA Avon sub-committee – had established some credibility for instituting repairs to Strensham Lock, but at a cost of a further £1,103 which Barwell had also funded. What a start for any new undertaking!

During those spring and summer months there was other vital work to be done: the story needed to be told of what was planned for the river, people had to be made aware of how it was to happen and what was already happening. This meant obtaining the interest of national, regional and local newspapers, which sent journalists and photographers to the river valley; they had to be shown, on various sites, the work

LANT first council, July 1950. Back row, from left to right: R.E. England, Sir H.R. Kerr, J. Sanders, R.G. Burlingham, R.B. Purves, C.R.P. Raymer, H.A.C. Freeman. Middle row: B.C. Cobb, K. Gill Smith, N.F. Davies, S.J. Grove, J.M. Smythe, E. Wright, H. Haden, W.J. Beecham. Front row: H. Ashwin, W.A. Bedford, G.S.D. Aldrich, C.D. Barwell, P.H. Protheroe, E.A. Goodland, R.F. Aickman, F.H. Knight. Absent: seven members.

required, and detailed explanations given of the reasons behind the whole enterprise. The BBC also arranged an outside radio broadcast (no television in those days!) which in turn attracted more press interest. Any opportunity – attendance at regattas and similar gatherings – was used to spread the word that at last something was being done about the Avon. A letter to *The Times* in August, followed by letters to *The Daily Telegraph* and to regional and local newspapers some weeks later, and 4,000 letters addressed to selected recipients launched a national appeal for £20,000, very roughly £280,000 in current values. Money began to trickle in and by November over £1,000 had been received – at least it was a start.

Membership of the Trust was by annual subscription. The minimum subscription was set at half a guinea (ten shillings and sixpence), but most members paid more, and covenanted their subscriptions so that the Trust could reclaim tax. The overall number of members was considered important as a way of attracting more interest and more new members.

A number of other and varied jobs were done: a scale of charges for pleasure craft was established, and although it had no mandatory force, was generally accepted: boat users

First appeal brochure, 1950.

felt that what they paid was now being used for their benefit. The lock-keeper at Avon Lock, Tewkesbury, whose only reward was the rent free occupation of the very decrepit lock cottage, had a new cooking range and calor gas lighting installed. Investigations were made into the purchase of the old mill cottage at Strensham for later conversion to a lock-keeper's house. And then there was endless correspondence to handle which grew as the general publicity took effect.

Probably as important as any of these tasks was the selection of like-minded enthusiastic people, both local and 'Brummie', each of whom could contribute an area of interest or expertise, and who would help run the new Trust and take an active part in the many and vital jobs to be done. Until now, it had been a largely single-handed effort by Barwell, who also had his own business to run.

So ended 1950 – a year of achievement: the Navigation bought and in safe hands; a new company formed to restore the Navigation; one lock already restored; an appeal launched and money starting to trickle in; key people recruited and, vitally, credibility beginning to be established. Solid progress indeed. A good start.

Consolidation – 1951

Having established the Trust on a reasonably firm base, 1951 clearly had to be a year of

Nafford Lock, 1950. Rebuilding of lower adit wall by volunteers.

consolidation and planning for further moves forward; nothing more could be done until there was either money in the bank, or at least firm promises for it.

A good start to the year was the news that the Special Commissioners of the Inland Revenue were minded to grant charitable status to the Trust – confirmation was received in August. This move would exempt the new Trust from tax and would enable tax to be reclaimed from covenanted subscriptions.

Barwell spent considerable time during the year on public relations and publicity generally. At that time there were not many PR practitioners, and in any case the Trust could not afford their fees; so it was a matter of learning as you go.

In January, Richard Dimbleby, a nationally well-respected radio, and later television, personality, interviewed the Avon lock-keeper, Arch Collins, for the BBC *Down Your Way* programme, in which the Trust received 'generous mention'.

An ambitious, time consuming, but ultimately unsuccessful PR scheme was the establishment of summer combined coach and river trips, mostly originating from the Birmingham, Black Country and Coventry areas and beyond. The failure of the scheme was largely due to the mechanical unreliability of the trip boat used, and the amount of time and effort expended did not correspond to the amount of income generated.

Visits to selected influential people proved much more rewarding: most generous donations were made by the John Feeney Charitable Trust which gave £500 in April, the

W.A. Cadbury Trust which gave £500, and the C.H. Foyle Trust which donated £1,000 in November. There were also many smaller but very welcome gifts.

During the summer Harry Dumbleton, a keen and skilled amateur photographer and motor cruiser owner, became involved with the Trust's work. During the next decade, whenever he could, Dumbleton recorded on cinefilm much of the restoration work on the river. His film, parts of which have now been transferred to videotape forming a unique historic record, were to become an invaluable tool in the many lecture tours made by Barwell for fund-raising purposes.

In August the midlands branch of the IWA organised a Rally of Boats at Tewkesbury, attended by thirty-five boats of all kinds: '...a motley fleet – cabin cruisers, converted pontoons, an ex-Boom Defence tender, a veteran canal tug, holiday barges, eight venerable narrow boats, and many other and less identifiable craft – but all were newly painted and very tidy.' The rally involved a cruise upstream to Pershore bridge, and a visit from a BBC outside broadcast unit – all good publicity.

Excellent articles appeared in *Worcestershire Countryside, The Sphere, Illustrated* and, by local author John Moore, in *The Observer*. Every opportunity was taken to obtain a few column inches in the regional and local press. A modest display promoting the Trust was staged at the Evesham Rowing Club's annual regatta.

On the practical side there was diverse activity. By now the Trust had established a general policy guideline, which was to keep open and in good repair that part of the Navigation from Tewkesbury to Pershore which was still in use, to obtain from it what little income there was, and broadly to work upstream from Pershore as and when funds became available. The privately owned cruiser population, such as it was, and a hire cruiser fleet were largely based downstream from Pershore; *Pisgah* ran regularly with grain from Gloucester or Sharpness to Pershore Mill.

Work, by volunteer working parties, started at Nafford Lock, rebuilding the lower adit wall and other tasks. Following negotiations, Worcestershire County Council accepted liability for maintaining the pedestrian swing bridge over the lock.

Because there were a number of troublesome underwater obstructions in the locks, largely caused by loose and falling masonry from walls badly needing repair, during the summer months Barwell decided to teach himself to dive. He purchased the appropriate diving suit, weights and breathing apparatus. From time to time he was able to carry out simple underwater tasks, thereby saving much time and the cost of hiring a professional diver. These simple diving jobs could be quite spectacular, and the publicity created for the Trust was probably as valuable as the actual tasks achieved.

Also in November, the derelict miller's cottage and land adjacent to Strensham Lock was purchased, with the intention of converting it to house a lock-keeper when there was sufficient money available.

Several visits were made to Captain J.F. Bomford at Springhill Farm, Fladbury. He, or his associated businesses, owned much riparian land between Evesham and Pershore, in particular that which gave land access to Fladbury and Chadbury locks. Captain Bomford was very co-operative, giving access consent when and where it was required.

In July there was a serious problem at Avon Lock at Tewkesbury. The top sluice became jammed, making the lock inoperable. It should be explained at this point that the top

Fladbury Lock, 1951. Barwell diving.

sluice of this lock is unusual anyway, and unique on the Avon. It comprises a horizontal frame and slide in the floor of the lock, immediately upstream of the top gates, which controls water flow to a culvert beneath the top gates and top cill; it is operated by a horizontal rod attached to a pivotted crank set inside the upper adit wall. Such positioning makes it inaccessible without either diving or dewatering. Fortunately DIWE had divers working at Upper Lode Lock on the river Severn nearby, who were able to be on site quickly. They discovered that the slide had disintegrated and jammed in the culvert hole and that the frame was broken. Three days later the divers fitted the repaired frame and a new slide; the lock was working once more.

However, the condition of the lower gates at Avon Lock was also giving concern. Their condition was beyond repair and new gates – as at Strensham the previous year – were the only sensible solution; furthermore they were the largest gates on the river and their replacement would be consequently expensive. Tewkesbury people would have to be asked to organise a local fund-raising appeal for 'their' lock.

★★★★★

The Barrow family, owners of Cropthorne Mill, were concerned at the very weak state of the decaying planks in the top gates at Fladbury lock. If these failed, the three mile long reach between Fladbury and Chadbury could drain, leaving a shallow muddy stream.

After discussions with them, when the Trust policy of working upstream from Pershore was explained, they expressed disappointment and concern that early attention could not be given to Fladbury lock. A compromise was reached: they gave an immediate £250, if the Trust would undertake unspecified preventative works. Quick thinking was needed to ensure a prompt response to justify the gift. It was decided to install a timber stank (temporary dam) in order to isolate the top gates from the river. This meant removal – largely by hand shovel – of large amounts of silted mud and vegetation, to expose the top gates. Several weekend volunteer working parties, involving up to ten people on occasions and as few as two on others, were needed. Among those involved were B.W. Thompson, F.W. Allen, D.V.S. Cottrell, R. Ede-England and C.R.P. Raymer, most of whom feature later in this story. I was also attracted to Fladbury at this time, perhaps seeing it as an opportunity to indulge in childhood dreams of playing with mud and water, albeit on a larger scale and in a more grown up way. I was fortunate in having some practical engineering skills which could be put to immediate use. In spite of delays caused by floods the stank was duly installed and by the following January, 1952, the rotten part of the gate planking was replaced, and the gift duly earned.

At Evesham, concern was being expressed at the weak and decayed state of the top gates at Chadbury Lock – the lock chamber and lower gates were completely derelict. Evesham staged a large and renowned annual regatta each Whit Monday and was proud to be known as 'the Henley of the Midlands'. There were also a number of tripping boats, including the steamer *Gaiety* and many rowing boats and punts for hire. If Chadbury Lock gates collapsed, the river at Evesham – a very attractive feature of the town – would revert to a shallow muddy stream. Not only would that be unattractive, there could be a potential health hazard as well. There was even talk of putting a permanent dam across the lock mouth.

In March, through Trust Council member K. Gill-Smith, also a director and leader writer of the locally influential *Evesham Journal* (and grandson of the chairman of the 1905 restoration proposals), Barwell was introduced to Brigadier H.H. Blanchard, an Evesham man with great knowledge and love of the Avon and former neighbour of Gill-Smith. The Brigadier was part of the 'top brass' at the War Office, and suggested that part of the Lower Avon restoration could form a useful training exercise for engineer soldiers. He put Barwell in touch with the Commanding Officer of No.1 Engineer Stores Depot, at Long Marston near Stratford-upon-Avon. The Royal Engineers expressed general interest and visited various potential sites on the river during the following months. By November they had progressed as far as saying they would like to undertake a field exercise at Chadbury Lock in the summer of 1952.

Barwell held talks with the Mayor of Evesham in November, on the need for locally raised funds to support any proposed work at Chadbury Lock. In July he had held talks with G.R. Speed – shortly to become chairman of the Appeals Committee – on methods and people who might be involved in fund-raising.

The first Annual General Meeting of The Lower Avon Navigation Trust Limited was held on 29 November at the Town Hall, Evesham. The Chairman's formal report for the year lists end of year (31 July 1951) membership of approximately 450 and income from subscriptions and donations of over £4,000, and a promise of £1,000 from the Borough of

Avon Lock Tewkesbury, 1952. The lower gate before removal and replacement. The lock cottage is in the background.

Evesham towards work at Chadbury Lock. Barwell had been repaid the monies he had provided both for the purchase of the Navigation and for the new lock gates at Strensham; the overall cost of the Strensham lock works – including two pairs of lock gates – was recorded as £1,650. Sir Reginald Kerr, Vice-Chairman of the Trust, had produced a very useful report on the whole Navigation, and formed an Operating Committee responsible for the operational working of that part of the Navigation which could be used. G.R. Speed, chairman of the Appeals and Public Relations Committee, had been planning future fund-raising projects. An order had been placed for new downstream lock gates for Avon Lock, Tewkesbury at an estimated cost of £2,000. Altogether, 1951 was a year of solid achievement with indications of a busy year ahead.

Fladbury Lock, 1951. Volunteer working party clearing silt and vegetation upstream of the top gates.

Chadbury Lock, 1952. The top and middle rails of the top gate are missing, with no support for the rapidly disintegrating gate planks.

3 Progress at Chadbury and Avon Locks; the Annuity

With substantial potential activity identified at Avon Lock, Tewkesbury and at Chadbury Lock, it was clear that the first priorities for 1952 would be fund-raising for these two projects.

In the early months Barwell, supported by Dumbleton with his cinefilm projector and screen, gave several lectures up and down the Avon valley. Every opportunity was taken to spread the word about the work of the Trust, collect funds, and persuade others to collect on the Trust's behalf.

In Evesham and the surrounding area a 'Save the Avon' campaign with a target of £4,000, specifically for Chadbury Lock, was very ably organised by G.R. Speed. An encouraging start was the promise of £1,000 from Evesham Borough Council. At that time the Borough Council had to obtain specific approval from the Ministry of Housing and Local Government to use ratepayers' funds in this way; that they did so, reflected the official civic enthusiasm for the scheme. Incidentally, this contribution remained the only direct public funding for the entire restoration project of the Lower Avon, except for a £200 grant from Worcestershire County Council in 1960. Local Authority powers to make grants of this sort just did not exist.

At its peak Evesham's 'Save the Avon' campaign involved over fifty local organisations, each with its fund-raising part to play, including a civic ball given by the Mayor of Evesham, and a carnival week culminating in a spectacular illuminated procession of boats, which alone raised over £950.

In the Tewkesbury area, fund-raising was less enthusiastic, with correspondingly smaller results. Nevertheless donations arrived from many places, including the first large covenanted subscription of over £1,000.

March saw a Trust stand at the National Trades Exhibition at Bingley Hall, Birmingham, the space having been given by the exhibition organisers.

Volunteer working parties were active during most weekends at Strensham. Regular workers included E. Haden, A. Minshaw, Sir R. Kerr, F.W. Allen and R. Harris. They cleared the area around the derelict miller's cottage, depositing and laying many hundreds of barrow loads of rubble in the muddy lane leading from Eckington to the lock. Further repair works were also done to the lock walls. At that time, because of shortages of building materials, no new building or major repairs could be done without a Building Licence. A licence to restore the cottage and make it habitable was obtained in April. A lock-keeper, D.R. Jones, with his wife, was appointed and installed in June, and continued to serve there until September 1968 when he retired at the age of seventy-five.

The Trust could not afford to pay its lock keepers or any other staff. (The Trust Secretary, E.J. Price, received a nominal honorarium – no other payments were made.) To overcome this problem the Trust decided to look for 'waterways enthusiasts' who would be willing to act as a lock-keepers – a seven day week with very long hours in season – in return for rent free accommodation. There was no shortage of applicants. The principle of the scheme still applies to Lower Avon lock-keepers forty-eight years later!

In March Barwell had his own business engagements in London, so he took the opportunity of visiting the Ministry of Transport (Docks and Canals Section) to 'seek co-operation' in obtaining permits to buy 5 tons of steel piling, so that the Trust could have a reserve stock for use in emergencies.

With every indication that the Royal Engineers would be doing work, as yet unspecified, at Chadbury Lock later in the year, Barwell asked me in February if I would form a small local group to oversee such operations. This was a great challenge and a wonderful opportunity for a relatively inexperienced twenty-two year old engineer. I lived and worked locally, and was able to organise my own work and the Trust's requirements to fit. Barwell also invited me to join the Trust Council, replacing my elder brother who was a first subscriber to the Memorandum and Articles.

A Chadbury Lock Works Sub-Committee (CLSC) was soon formed, comprising B.W. Thompson, Consulting Engineer and Chairman of the Trust's Works Committee; G.J. Bomford, managing director of a local building and civil engineering business; T.R. Bateman, architect; R.J. Madge, surveyor for Evesham Rural District Council; A.L. Tuckwood, retired building contractor; F. Preece, plant hire contractor; S.J. Grove, local steam boat proprietor; R.B. Purves, local riparian owner of Chadbury weir and other land. Collectively this group had a wealth of experience and expertise.

Soon after the CLSC was formed it came to my notice that arrangements had been made much earlier to use the services of a Consulting Engineer. This seemed to me to conflict with the necessity of having the group we had just formed. (See Appendix D.)

The CLSC's first task was to agree with the local Building Trades Unions and Building Trade Employers that the Trust could use soldiers, instead of their members, on this particular job. This was a War Office requirement (A.C.I.56 19 January 1952).

Agreement was then reached with the Royal Engineers on the scope of their short field exercise. The whole structure would be isolated by driving piles across both ends; the lock dewatered by pumping, and all mud and debris removed to enable a thorough inspection to be made. Remember that all that was known about the condition of the structure was that which could be seen above water level. After inspection, decisions could be made about what work was necessary and how it should be done. Troops would then be withdrawn from site for some months, to enable works to be done by others.

Chadbury Lock was a 'diamond' lock, with a diamond shaped lock chamber, like Wyre Lock today. There are many theories about the reasons for building locks this shape: possibly the original lock chamber was turf sided, having masonry only at each end to support the lock gates, probably less costly than masonry throughout; there may have been originally special ground configuration considerations; we just do not know.

On 19 May, having received a civic welcome in Evesham en route, the Royal Engineers arrived at Chadbury Lock. They comprised a core of regular and national service experienced tradesmen, under day to day command of a very experienced Warrant Officer First Class, and a much larger group of supplementary reservists – called up for two weeks each year. Their Officers, based at Long Marston depot, made frequent visits to site. They arrived in nineteen trucks, with assorted heavy plant and a Bailey bridge. Camp was set up at the back of the lock-

Chadbury Lock, 1952. Royal Engineers pile off the upstream end.

side field to be above flood level – a very wise precaution as it turned out.

Caught up in the general euphoria which accompanied the arrival of the Royal Engineers to save the Avon, without reference to the CLSC, Barwell told the main group of soldiers that the Trust would provide one pint of beer per man per day. After all, there were only twelve or fourteen men, who would only be on site for two or three weeks at most. The soldiers selected a preferred hostelry and payments were duly made. As it turned out the two or three weeks became forty one weeks, which added up to quite a lot of beer! Even so, it was a much lower cost than employing a civil engineering contractor. This item is listed as 'subsistences "Chequers"' in the costings in Appendix F. The matter was not discussed publicly at the time!

By mid-June, the lock was dewatered and cleared, and an inspection was made on 16 June. Overall the condition was much worse than expected. The only really sound parts were the underwater portions of the upstream adit walls. All the remainder was either dubious, bad, or simply non-existent.

The CLSC was now faced with two problems: the imminent withdrawal of the soldiers and their equipment from site, and the uncertainty of how much money would be available and when. The Evesham Appeal was going well, but the major fund-raising events were not due to take place until August. It was clearly essential to secure the upstream end of the lock at the very least. Detailed specifications would have to be prepared and tenders sought from suitable contractors.

Then came the best news of all. The Royal Engineers had so benefited from their exercise that they asked if they could stay on and do the whole job, subject to approval by the War Office, the Trust being responsible for the procurement of and payment for all

Chadbury Lock, 1952. The condition of the lock chamber walls is revealed. Note the downstream cill in the foreground and the vertical wooden quoin.

material used. The answer was simple – yes please! The sting, of course, was in the tail: subject to War Office approval!

However there was a degree of preparation work which could be progressed while the formal Approval was processed. This was the first time that armed forces had been used for a civilian aid project of this nature; troops had been used many times to give emergency help to local authorities and the police, but not to a charitable Navigation Authority restoring a derelict piece of industrial archaeology! There was no precedent at all for this and therefore no rules 'in the book' to guide those making the decision. Doubtless the buck was passed from section to section and committee to committee, because it was not until three months later, in mid-September, that official approval to proceed was received. A dry, warm summer which would have been perfect for civil engineering works had turned into autumn.

One advantage of this delay was that there was now sufficient money for the Trust to authorise expenditure – up to £2,000 initially – on materials. This was one of the CLSC's tasks – obtaining the requisite licences and permits for reinforcement steel, shuttering and other timber, and scheduling deliveries of these materials, aggregates and cement to site. Knowing the lead time for delivery of materials, and bearing in mind that some were in very short supply, I tried to visit the site daily, so that requirements were anticipated well in advance, and could be delivered as and when required. A supply of spring water near the soldiers' camp was

Chadbury Lock, 1952. Preparation for rebuilding. Demolition of unsound downstream walls. Note the cross beams for the original downstream end floor planks and cill.

analysed and found to be suitable for concrete making: river water was too dirty. Contingency arrangements had to be in place for alternative delivery sites when access routes were flooded, to ensure that work was not delayed. During the waiting time all demolition of unsound masonry was completed, the rubble being used to make a compacted base in the lock bottom on which new work could be based. Drains were also laid in the base to enable the whole, which was roughly 9ft below top river level, to be kept dry by continuous pumping.

With financial confidence secure, a decision was made to rebuild the lock chamber as parallel sided, and to rebuild the whole downstream end. A pair of new upstream lock gates was ordered for late autumn delivery.

Work proceeded throughout the autumn and early winter months. Reinforced concrete upstream adit walls were constructed on the original sound masonry base; the upstream cill was replaced precisely where the original was sited (although it was discovered, some years later, that this made the lock too short for full length narrow boats); upstream quoins (the hollows in which the lock gates pivot) were cast in concrete integral with the completely new whole mass structure of lock floor, walls, downstream cill and quoins. Materials quantities are given in Appendix F.

Floods disrupted work twice; early snow and blizzards made working conditions difficult. By December the access track across the field from the approach lane and camp to the lock site was only passable on a marked route, and some heavy plant was bogged down for several days, mud in places being 4ft 6in deep.

During the summer Barwell had reached an agreement with the very helpful DIWE that when the Trust required straightforward lock gate construction, installation and maintenance, they would allow their very experienced foreman, W.G. Munn, and their tradesmen to work directly for the Trust in their spare time at evenings and weekends, the

Chadbury Lock, 1952. Reinforcement steel for new parallel sided lock rises from the new lock floor. Note the old diamond shaped lock chamber behind the reinforcement steel. In the background on the bridge are D.H. Burlingham and WO1 J. Loach.

Trust paying them direct. Rates of pay were agreed for 1952 at 4/6d an hour for the foreman and 4/- an hour for tradesmen, irrespective of hours worked. In 1953 these rates were increased to 4/9d and 4/3d respectively.

New upstream lock gates were installed in early January 1953 and the downstream cills fitted to enable new gates, when made, to be installed without having to dewater the lock. Construction work was now complete and the pumps were stopped on 21 January, allowing the lock to flood. All that remained to be done was the making and installation of downstream gates, with balance arms and paddle gear for all four gates, and extraction of the pile cofferdam at both ends of the lock.

The state of the field was so bad that the owners, J.M. Stokes Ltd, asked the Trust to withdraw from the site as soon as practicable. The pile cofferdams were extracted, and all plant was withdrawn and the camp dismantled by 26 February after forty-one consecutive weeks on site. The lane from Ryden Farm, Charlton to the site and the field itself were later reinstated when conditions allowed.

During the summer new downstream lock gates were made at Diglis workshops, Worcester, and taken by road to site. They were installed during July, together with paddle gear made to the original Lower Avon pattern – the only lock on the river to be so equipped.

Barwell was very keen that all new repaired woodwork and ironwork on the Navigation should be well painted with bitumen paint; this was a job that occupied many volunteers.

Chadbury Lock, 1953, as completed by No.1 ESD Royal Engineers. Note that only top gates have been fitted, and that treadwalks and mooring ballards have been installed with a plinth for the official plaque. Bottom gates, balance arms and paddle gear were fitted later.

Not only did it look smart, in theory it should also protect these materials with an impermeable covering.

Timber is an organic material; any moisture trapped between the timber surface and the impermeable skin would start to decay the timber. If wet, timber must be able to dry out. I pointed this out to Barwell, saying that I thought it unwise to treat new timber, and particularly the new gates, with bitumen paint; and that creosote, which is fungicidal and penetrated timber without forming a skin, would be a far better and longer lasting preservative. Barwell did not accept this, and neither did I accept his insistence on using bitumen paint. The upshot was: 'If you want the Chadbury gates creosoted, you b….. well do it yourself.' So I did.

Of all the timber lock gates on the Lower Avon, those at Chadbury, made and installed forty-seven years ago, if properly maintained, are good for a least another decade. Other bitumen painted lock gates on the river, made very many years later, have not survived. I rest my case!

A formal opening ceremony took place on 1 August in front of a large crowd. Accompanied by the Mayor of Evesham, Councillor J.M. Hodges, who had been very supportive of the whole project, Sir Raymond Priestley, Vice-Chancellor of Birmingham University, cut a tape and unveiled a plaque. Later S.J. Groves' steamer *Gaiety* made an inaugural trip from Evesham through the lock to Fladbury.

The whole Chadbury project was a great success. The overall cost of £3,993 5s 2d (see Appendix F) was met entirely from funds raised with great enthusiasm by many individuals and organisations in Evesham and district and the £1,000 donation from Evesham Borough Council. The fact that armed forces (Royal Engineers) were closely involved attracted valuable national publicity and gave added credence to the Trust.

The Royal Engineers Journal Vol. LXVII of September 1953 gives an account of the lock reconstruction. Among several conclusions is 'Our civilian colleagues can teach us a thing or two about ensuring a job does not get held up for stores.'

★★★★★

Back now to 1952 and the other projects carried out during the summer. In September the new downstream gates for Avon Lock, Tewkesbury were completed and the DIWE, as main contractor for the job, moved them by water from Worcester together with a floating crane. There were no downstream stank slots – the large grooves in the lock walls outside the lock gates into which large timber baulks could be slotted to make a temporary stank or dam. This meant that the downstream end of the lock mouth had to be dammed, by driving a row of steel piles, to dewater the lock chamber for fitting the gates and other very necessary underwater repairs. The piled cofferdam was successfully driven, and during the next stage, the construction of a temporary bridge/working platform across the lock, a slipping rope caused the floating crane to capsize in 9ft of water. However, recovery was rapidly achieved, the new gates installed and other essential repair works done, all within six days – a remarkable achievement by any standards. The cost of the work was £2,850, a disappointingly small part of which was raised locally.

During October a further development occurred in the saga of the £400 Annuity, which was specifically excluded from the sale of the old Lower Avon Navigation Company to Barwell in 1950. A.C. Lisle, the Executive Divisional Manager of DIWE, the ultimate successors to the proprietors of the Stratford-upon-Avon Canal, said that he could no longer authorise payment of the Annuity to Whitehouse, as he was no longer proprietor of the Lower Avon Navigation. He advised Barwell to seek legal advice. Accordingly, accompanied by Lisle, Barwell consulted Sir Theodore Pritchett of Hatwell, Pritchett & Co. in Birmingham. It was subsequently agreed that DIWE would cease making payments to Whitehouse and would make them instead to the Lower Avon Navigation Trust as proprietors of the Lower Avon Navigation. The Trust would place the payments in a separate suspense account, and would not use them until settlement of any impending dispute with Whitehouse.

At Strensham Lock, volunteer working parties continued to clear the site and make a lock-side garden. During November a mains water supply was laid from Jackson's farm at Eckington to the lock-side, a distance of almost three quarters of a mile. While the trenching was done by contractor, the fitting and lagging of the galvanised steel pipe was all done by volunteer labour.

So ended 1952. Substantial sums of money raised and spent. The 'front door' to the Navigation at Avon Lock, Tewkesbury secured. A lock-keeper installed in a restored cottage with mains water supply at Strensham. Chadbury Lock substantially completed – waiting only for new lower gates to be made and fitted the following year. Positive moves made regarding the Annuity. Much valuable publicity gained, both locally, regionally and nationally from successful progress. Very many people aware of and involved with the Trust's work in some way. A good year.

Chadbury Lock, 1953 – fitting balance arms to the newly installed bottom gates. All balance arm timbers were manhandled into position, and the mortice and tenon joints cut by hand on site.

Avon Lock, Tewkesbury, 1952. New bottom gates fitted. The steam powered floating crane is in the background.

Chadbury Lock, 1953. The formal reopening by Sir Raymond Priestly MC, MA, DSc.

4 Wyre and Pershore Locks

February 1953 saw the beginning of the Trust's long association with Wyre Mill, when that five-acre property, comprising a large four-floor mill building, house, dam with paddle-type sluice and two weirs, came on the market. The association between the Trust and Wyre Mill lasted twenty-eight years and, while it is peripheral to the main story, it is important, and more easily told at this stage than spread piecemeal over the years.

Despite the fact that the condition of the buildings was very run down, the main dam was in need of essential repairs, the sluice was in a state of collapse, and there was a large and growing weir scour hole, the medium and long term potential for the property was enormous, and its control was a very attractive proposition for the Trust. Barwell's thinking was that with immediate and modest adaptation the property could become a very useful base for Trust activities, while at the same time allowing access for essential repairs to the dam, sluice and weirs; the mill property was not part of the Navigation, but could be very useful to it. It was a once-in-a-lifetime opportunity to purchase, so after appropriate appraisal, an offer to purchase was made, which was accepted in November.

Trust funds, such as they were, were insufficient and in any case could not be used for this project, so Barwell, together with other active and staunch Trust supporters including F.W. Allen, T.R. Burrowes, T.R. Bateman, G.W. Mathews, D.C.B. Mathews and R. Harrison, financed the purchase of Wyre Mill Productions Ltd which owned the whole property.

Mains water and electricity supply were laid on to the property, and volunteer working parties soon started working to adapt parts of the house and mill for use as a Club with basic overnight accommodation. Members were recruited both for the new Club and the Trust, their physical contribution to working parties being valued as much as their membership subscription. Part of the land was used as a caravan site for members and part for mooring their boats; other parts were used by the Trust for storage. Gradually Wyre Mill Club became firmly established, with an ongoing programme of improvements that in turn attracted more members. This membership provided a very useful source of Trust workers and supporters. Members of the Club were strongly persuaded to join and actively support the work of the Lower Avon Navigation Trust.

By 1960, Wyre Mill Productions Ltd was in a position to satisfy Barwell's original intention that the Trust should own the property. Accordingly the freehold was passed to the Trust. The funding of the purchase price was achieved by a very complex arrangement between Wyre Mill Club and the Trust, of mortgages and rental, which at the end of twenty-one years would leave the Trust in sole possession of the property. A small part of the site was not leased to Wyre Mill Club but was retained by the Trust for development as a maintenance wharf. Under the terms of the lease, the Trust was responsible for maintenance of the weirs, sluice and main dam, of which it now had the freehold; repairs

Wyre Weir, 1954. The weir has been dried off to expose the scoured hole. The clay core with stone-on-edge capping can be clearly seen.

to the buildings were the responsibility of the tenant, Wyre Mill Club.

On expiry of the lease in 1981 the Trust sold the property, at valuation agreed by the Charity Commissioners, to Wyre Mill Club Ltd, retaining the land used as a maintenance wharf. The sale provided a useful capital base for the Trust and gave the Club incentive to invest in its own property.

Over the years Wyre Mill has been, and continues to be, a very valuable centre for the Trust's volunteer working parties, and a local Avon base for its members who live away from the area. A strong informal association continues between the Mill and the Trust.

★★★★★

1953 generally had to be a time of consolidation and planning ahead. The next large scale task on the Navigation was the restoration of the derelict Wyre Lock, then the limit of navigation upstream, for which funds would have to be raised before any work could be done.

It was at this time, through R.F. Aickman, founder and Vice-President of the Inland Waterways Association, a first subscriber to Trust's Articles and Memorandum and a member of its Council, that Barwell was introduced to Captain V. Bulkeley-Johnson, then Hon. Treasurer of IWA and associated with a wealthy City charitable trust named 'The Mrs Smith Trust'. Captain and Mrs. Bulkeley-Johnson were about to take a canal and river holiday on their cruiser, and were to visit the Severn and Avon. To quote Barwell's diary

> ...the scene was set, the opportunity to seek their Trust's financial aid imminent and the need for me to meet and consolidate his (Bulkeley-

Johnson's) thinking in our direction was of top priority. Eventually his arrival at Avon Lock was reported to me…The outcome can only be described as satisfactory…we were able to provide transportation to shops, also to several of our locks and their surroundings.

In June 'The Mrs. Smith Trust' gave £500, and later asked that the Lower Avon Navigation Trust should nominate a specific task for them to support. This offer appeared to provide security for funds needed for the Wyre Lock restoration, although it was planned to raise them through a local Appeal. An acceptable suggestion was made to 'The Mrs. Smith Trust' that they might consider funding some form of modification to Pershore Watergate. A very useful contact had been made.

An Appeal Committee with H.T. Horton as chairman and Mr. and Mrs. Max Phipps as joint secretaries for Pershore and District was established in April to raise funds for the Wyre Lock restoration. Their principal activities would be concentrated during the following year, although a rally of boats was planned for August and a formal start in the autumn.

Wyre Lock was, and still is, 'diamond' in shape: the length between gates is approximately 74ft, and at its widest the lock chamber width is approximately 49ft.

A preliminary survey of the lock was made in March 1953, which showed that the upstream lock gates were repairable by replanking, the downstream gates had completely rotted away at water level, parts of the lock chamber walls would need rebuilding, other parts appeared sound. The whole lock chamber was completely silted up, trees and other vegetation were growing from the walls and part of the upstream approach channel was almost solid land! There were also ancillary problems on adjacent property not owned by the Trust, in the form of scoured channels in the dam by the lock, a bad scour hole in one of the weirs and collapsed sluices by Wyre Mill.

A further complication was that a large part of the island between the lock and the river was owned by J. Whitehouse, the former director of the Lower Avon Navigation Company, from whom Barwell had purchased the Navigation and with whom the Trust was now in dispute over the Annuity. This comparatively small parcel of land was specifically excluded from the 1950 purchase. The immediate consequence was that all work on the island side of the lock would have to be tackled from within the lock chamber, and there could be absolutely no access onto Whitehouse's land.

Detailed planning was done during the early autumn, shortly after the formal reopening of Chadbury Lock, so that invitations to tender for the job could be sent out to civil engineering contractors. A small works sub-committee, similar to that at Chadbury, was set up to plan and oversee the work. It comprised C.D. Barwell, Trust Chairman, T.R. Bateman, architect, E.S. Goodall, engineer, local businessman and a very active fund raiser for Chadbury, J.L. Sanders, boatbuilder from Pershore, H.T. Horton, chairman of Pershore Appeal, and me as chairman. With the experience of Chadbury Lock restoration behind them, they felt sufficiently confident to decide what had to be done and to negotiate with contractors and others.

They decided to have two separate contracts: one for piling off, dewatering and clearing the lock, and subsequently draglining the upstream approach channel. Works later found to be necessary would be the subject of negotiation, as would ancillary works on adjacent

Wyre Lock, 1953. The upstream approach channel is silted up.

Wyre Lock, 1954. The lock is dewatered, showing its 'diamond' shape. Parts of the lock and the chamber walls are in poor condition, the top gates and cills are suitable for repair. This lock had no floor; walls built on timber piles were protected by random stone.

property. The second contract would be for repairs to and replanking of the upstream lock gates and for making and installing new downstream gates. These works would be done by Foreman Munn and his gang working for the Trust in their own time, the Trust being responsible for purchase of materials. Invitations to tender for the first contract were sent out to seven contractors with a return date of 15 January 1954.

★★★★★

January 1953 saw the publication to Trust members of the first issue of *Avon News*, a duplicated, four-page 'modest journal wherein we can more frequently and in an informal manner communicate to all concerned our views and intentions…' A total of ninety-six issues of *Avon News* have been published over the years, most issues being printed and carrying photographs. In 1992 *Avon News* was succeeded by the *Avon Bulletin,* of which thirty-six issues have been published. (to January 1999).

During August bank holiday weekend a Coronation rally for boats was held at Pershore Recreation Ground and adjoining meadows. Seventy-six boats attended, some having travelled 'hundreds of miles', the longest distance being 307 miles. There was a Sunday Service at which the Assistant Bishop of Worcester, the Rt. Revd C.E. Stuart preached.

To get to and from the rally site, craft had to pass through Pershore Watergate. R. Harrison has recorded his recollections of how this was done:

> The procedure we used to do was that all the boats going up would arrive before eight o'clock at night. (They would moor to the bank between the Watergate and Pershore road bridge, opposite J. Sanders' moorings). At eight o'clock the gang (boats crews) would winch the gate to and Jim Sanders (who lived opposite) would lower the lashers, the paddles, and then we would all go to sleep. At nine o'clock the next morning the river would be up sufficiently for us to get into Pershore Lock. So up we go to various functions, rallies and what not.
>
> Then we had to come down again. So we would all go down and collect round the gate and would winch the gate open. And then the gang would stand either side of the gate (opening) with fend offs and things as the various vessels came down. Some went through bow first, some went backwards, some went broadside, some hit both sides. So it was quite a hair-raising expedition to do that.

So 1953 was a less eventful year, but one of busy, firm consolidation.

Wyre Lock restoration and planning for Pershore Lock – 1954
C.R.P. Raymer, accountant and Trust Assistant Treasurer, joined the Wyre Lock sub-committee to inspect the tenders for the lock restoration which were received in January 1954. After negotiations, that of Thomas Vale & Sons Ltd, of Stourport, was accepted. This firm later undertook various other jobs for the Trust. They were always prepared to extend credit, when at a time of unpredictable fund-raising it was difficult to forecast cash flow accurately.

E.S. Goodall negotiated land access for the contractors to the lock site through Wick. A start on site was made in May and the sub-committee inspected the dewatered lock on 1 June, accepting Vales' prices for additional repair works then revealed, which largely comprised rebuilding in reinforced concrete two large sections of lock wall. The upstream cills were considered satisfactory by Foreman Munn, but the downstream cills and the wooden floor to which they were fixed would require renewal. Work proceeded satisfactorily during the following weeks, although the site was completely flooded and work had to stop on four occasions: twice in June and twice in August. The ancillary works on adjacent property were also completed. An analysis of costs for the whole job is given in Appendix G.

A formal reopening ceremony took place on 12 September, a tape being cut by Miss Beryl Foyle, a trustee of the very supportive C.H. Foyle Trust. Over one thousand people attended the occasion and were ferried across the river from Wyre, thus giving splendid publicity for further fund-raising. Afterwards twenty-five boats made the journey to Cropthorne Watergate, the new extended limit of navigation.

In December 1953, the Severn River Board, whose Avon Improvement Scheme works were now only a few miles from Pershore, approached Barwell and offered to 'dredge away' Pershore Watergate as part of their overall scheme. The watergate was a very cumbersome apparatus to operate, and could be described as an obstruction to straightforward travel on the river; the River Board clearly viewed it as an obstruction to land drainage. However, without its use there was insufficient depth of water to pass under Pershore Old Bridge and enter Pershore Lock, a mile upstream.

There were three possible navigation options. The first was to build a new pound lock on or near the site of the watergate; this would permanently raise the water level between it and Pershore Lock, thereby affecting both land drainage and the Pershore miller's head of water. (Pershore Mill used water powered turbines until its destruction by fire in July 1976.) This option was therefore unacceptable. The second possibility was to build a new lock chamber immediately below Pershore Lock, thereby making either a staircase lock (the lower chamber connecting directly to the upper chamber) or a double lock with a very short pound, with a probable maximum length of ten feet between. The third possibility was to deepen Pershore Lock. Both second and third options would require deepening the channel beneath Pershore Old Bridge.

The Mrs Smith Trust trustees had already indicated that they would support a properly considered solution to this problem, and the Severn River Board agreed to the principle of a new lock chamber or deepened lock in order to eliminate the current obstruction caused by the watergate.

Partridge's, the Pershore millers, who operated the grain barge *Pisgah,* also supported the principle, even though construction of any proposed solution would prevent their use of *Pisgah* for several months. *Pisgah's* normal journey time from Gloucester to Pershore Watergate – 29 miles – took approximately six hours; the journey from the watergate to the mill – one mile – took four hours under normal river conditions.

Around the turn of the year approaches were made by Barwell to the Royal Engineers to see if they would be able to offer any form of help. While expressing interest, they decided the scale of the task was too large for their available resources. In any event the

Wyre Lock, 1954. Partially cleared upstream approach channel, looking towards lock. Note the solidity of the silted material and the upstream pile cofferdam.

Wyre Lock, 1954. A replanked top gate is being installed. Note the method of lifting gates with manual winch operated block and tackle from a stayed single pole – adjustment of the stays changed the verticality of the lift. Nearly all gate installations were done this way.

Pershore Watergate, 1955. Illustrations to show difficulty of operation.

Gang awaiting arrival of Pisgah. *Extreme left is spill weir - then fixed lashers in open position, then the open navigation gate with paddles closed. Note the posts with snatch blocks and winch used to open and close the gate, and the wire cable to connect to* Pisgah.

Effect of 'fresh' water pouring through the navigation gate. Fixed lashers (paddles) open on right.

Pisgah *approaching. C.D. Barwell is in raincoat and gumboots, with his back to* Pisgah. *In front of Barwell, also in a raincoat, is G. Botteley.*

Pisgah *entering the navigation gate. Note the assisting winch operated cable. In the right foreground is the top beam of the navigation gate..*

Pisgah *further into navigation gate. Her position secure, the assisting gang can be more relaxed.*

Pisgah *almost through the navigation gate, but still using the foredeck winch to cable secured to riverbank 100ft upstream.*

trade unions were now opposed to the use of troops in this way.

So, what should be done? Resolution of this particular problem was likely to be very costly, and was beyond the experience of amateur civil engineers – professional help was clearly required. B.W. Thompson, chairman of the Trust's Works Committee, introduced Mr G. Botteley of Botteley and Chaffer, consulting Civil Engineers of Sutton Coldfield, to the Trust. During the spring and early summer Botteley conducted a very thorough site survey and investigation, including an inspection by a diver of the underwater footings of Pershore Old Bridge, which was a scheduled Ancient Monument in the care of The Office of Works.

With a professional diver on site, Worcestershire County Council Highways and Bridges department asked if they could use the diver's services at the adjacent Pershore New Bridge (in 1926 the first reinforced concrete bridge to be constructed in Worcestershire) and share the cost with the Trust.

The change in the facial expressions of the County Council bridge engineers when the diver walked right under one end of one of the New Bridge piers, the footings of which, unknown to anybody, had been washed away, was very memorable! The diving inspections had proved useful for both the County Council and the Trust.

Botteley's site investigations also included bore holes in and immediately downstream of Pershore Lock to obtain information regarding the ground conditions for a good depth below the lock floor and river bed.

In July 1954, a Pershore Lock Reconstruction Committee (PLRC) was set up with Barwell as chairman, including T.R. Burrowes, E.S. Goodall, R. Sankey-Smith, B.W. Thompson and me as deputy chairman and secretary. As Botteley obtained information from his investigations, he would hold discussions with PLRC so that together we could think through the problems and possible solutions. By the end of the year, PLRC had considered recommendations to put before the Trust Council at its January 1955 meeting.

In January 1954 the Pershore 'Save the Avon' Appeal Committee launched an ambitious programme with a target of £2,000. Events included square dancing, a comic cricket match, a boxing display, a motor cycle gymkhana, a tug-o-war contest, dances, a street carnival, sailing races and a riverside church service. Many local organisations were involved, as were adjacent villages with dances, the choosing of an 'Avon Queen' and other events. These activities took place during the year, some under difficult weather conditions.

The summer and autumn of 1954 were the wettest for many years, causing extensive and frequent flooding; the A44 road at Pershore Bridge was flooded on one occasion and the lock-keepers at Avon Lock and Strensham Lock had to be evacuated.

Earlier in the year the Trust received a donation towards Wyre Lock of £400 from Ernest Thomas, Canal Boat Builder of Walsall, and with this gift also two 22ft long wooden pontoons made from sections of surplus narrow boat hulls. The pontoons were delivered to Tewkesbury and towed to Pershore Mill by *Pisgah*. Being square ended they were difficult to tow, but made ideal floating work platforms. They were used by Vales at Wyre Lock, and by others at other sites, towed by boat-owning Trust members.

So 1954 had been another busy year. Wyre Lock was restored and in use; a successful fund-raising appeal had been made in Pershore and district in spite of atrocious weather; extensive investigations were made for a possible major operation at Pershore, and all despite the wettest year for a long time.

Pershore Lock restoration and associated works

1955 began with a momentous decision by the Trust Council in February.

With the completion of Wyre Lock restoration the previous year, the river was navigable from Tewkesbury to Cropthorne Watergate, and from the derelict Fladbury Lock upstream to Evesham. Only Fladbury Lock, just under half a mile of river, and Cropthorne Watergate remained before the Trust's objective to restore the Navigation from 'Evesham to the sea' could be achieved. This was a very appealing thought, and a strongly supported one; its disadvantage was that with two watergates, the through journey would not be an easy one. The alternative proposition of deepening Pershore Lock, or constructing a new lock chamber immediately below the existing one, plus deepening beneath Pershore Old Bridge, deepening Fladbury Lock and removing Cropthorne Watergate was likely to be so costly that, even if the work could be done reasonably early, the financial consequences were likely to defer the Trust's ability to do further major works for some years.

The latter option had been very thoroughly discussed with Botteley by the PLRC. Their preferred option was to deepen Pershore Lock and the channel beneath Pershore Old Bridge and to remove the watergate; they had authorised tenders for the work to be obtained so there was a firm price known for the job, £11,746. The watergate would be removed at little or no cost to the Trust by the Severn River Board.

The PLRC made a very strong recommendation to the Trust Council that their preferred option should be adopted. There was a long and very exhaustive debate, at the end of which their recommendation was unanimously accepted.

The Trust's funding policy for works was that before orders were placed, at least half the estimated cost of the job had to be immediately available either in the bank or in the form of reasonably firm promises of support. The Trust was short of this requirement by over £3,000 – but within weeks sufficient further support from the C.H. Foyle Trust, the W.A. Cadbury Trust, the Mrs Smith Trust and various individuals was offered. Other generous members offered collateral security should loans be required.

The decision having been made, and with sufficient funds in place to start, the tender of Concrete Piling Company Ltd of London was formally accepted in March 1955.

Pershore Lock was a semi-diamond shaped lock and the distance across the diamond was much less than that at Wyre. To deepen it, two parallel rows of steel piles would be driven down the centre of the semi-diamond shaped lock chamber, and just over 4ft depth of lock floor excavated between the rows of piles. The downstream end of the lock would be completely rebuilt in reinforced concrete to take a new, deeper cill and new, deeper lock gates.

Access to the lock-side was from a 400 yard long private footpath, which narrowed to 2ft 6in wide past Pershore Mill. Heavy plant could only get to the site by making a ford across the weir channel, while the Severn River Board drew (emptied) the river by opening their flood control sluice gates at Nafford. Other smaller items travelled on *Pisgah* from Gloucester Docks to the lock-side. Aggregates, cement, reinforcing steel, piles, boiler coal (for the steam operated piling hammer) and all other materials had to be ferried across the mill stream on a floating pontoon from a builder's yard in Bridge Street, Pershore; several hundreds of tons in total, all having to be double handled on and off the ferry pontoon. It was not the easiest of sites for access!

Pershore Lock, 1955, dewatered before deepening. Its 'semi-diamond' shape and timber floor planks can be seen.

Pershore Lock, 1955. Parallel rows of piles can be seen with excavation work in between. The semi-diamond shape can be seen in the top right hand corner.

Pershore Lock, 1956. The breach between the weir discharge channel and the downstream lock approach channel is piled off. The piles are now almost completely buried by spoil. The 'gut' weir discharge channel can be seen behind the piles.

By the end of May all the equipment was on site, work began and continued for the next ten months. There were delays caused by bad weather, both floods and frosts, difficulty in recruiting local labour, and an unexpected quantity of large tipped stone on the line of the downstream cofferdam. Ferrous metals (including reinforcing steel and steel piles) had just been released from Government controls, leading to heavy demand and extended delivery dates. However, by the end of March 1956, the work was almost finished.

While Concrete Piling Ltd were on site with all their pile driving equipment, the opportunity was taken to pile off and seal a breach which had occurred some years earlier, between the weir discharge channel and the lock approach channel. Subsequent realignment of the approach channel has almost buried this long row of piles, some of which can still be seen from the footpath from the lower landing stage to the lock-side.

During the autumn months of 1955, Foreman Munn and his men constructed a new pair of downstream lock gates, which were delivered to the site by road to Pershore and by pontoon ferry to the lock-side in January.

In August Concrete Piling started work at Pershore Old Bridge. The whole centre arch channel had to be piled off and dewatered. To deepen the channel beneath the arch, the two bridge piers on either side had to be under-pinned, and the existing elm timber piles on which the piers were supported had to be carefully removed and replaced by temporary horizontal beams which also served to prevent any lateral movement. The elm piles, when removed, were as firm and sound as the day they were driven, some five hundred years earlier. After exposure to the air they crumbled to dust within three weeks.

Having temporarily secured the two bridge piers, excavation underneath the bridge could

Pershore Old Bridge, 1955. The centre navigation arch is piled off for deepening.

commence. A 5ft depth below the former level had to be very carefully dug out by hand, scrupulously observed by The Office of Works and the County Bridgemaster. A reinforced concrete invert – U-shaped – was then constructed, both to give a clear depth of water of 5ft at times of low flow, and to support the two bridge piers, the weight of which was now transferred to the underwater concrete floor. The job was completed by mid-October.

During the excavation a carved stone cross was uncovered, which caused great archaeological interest, and various claims were made about its origin and ownership. The cross was in the Almonry Museum at Evesham for many years, and was given by them to Pershore Heritage Centre in 1999.

In October, the Severn River Board started to demolish the watergate, which by mid-November had been removed to a few inches above water level. A Royal Engineer demolition unit – experts in controlled explosions – was engaged to shatter the underwater masonry for subsequent removal by dragline. Any use of explosives made good television news and publicity for the Trust. But on 20 December something went wrong. Instead of a gentle shattering of masonry, there was a tremendous explosion and debris was scattered over a wide area. Fortunately there were no casualties and very little damage.

While all this activity was taking place at Pershore, there was a temporary collapse at Nafford Lock. The planking on all the lock gates was so rotten that it was starting to fall apart and make the lock impossible to use. A temporary stoppage was made and each gate was lifted out in turn by block and tackle suspended from a single pole, re-planked and refitted. The job took five days.

Pershore Old Bridge, 1955. Manual excavations beneath the navigation arch are in progress. The men are filling buckets by hand, and on the right by the buckets an old timber pile is lying on the ground.

In April, with the vital need for fund-raising in mind, Barwell secured the services of F.J. Johnson, a professional journalist and publisher and recently retired managing director of *The Birmingham Gazette and Dispatch*. With excellent midlands contacts, he produced a steady stream of much needed financial support, as well as some excellent publicity. Unfortunately, only seven months later he had to resign due to ill health.

★★★★★

1956 began with the need to complete works at Pershore. This involved the installation of the new downstream lock gates and the dredging of the downstream approach channel to the lock.

In March the Trust was advised by the Severn River Board that they wished to deepen the discharge channel from their flood control sluices at Pershore and revet the river bank opposite to prevent erosion. This would involve the deepening of the lock approach channel. The Board's surveys showed that the new depth of the channel would need to be 4ft 6in deeper than it was already. The Severn River Board would include these works in their scheme, thereby saving the Trust a very considerable cost. The spoil removed, which was mostly gravel, could be used to reinforce the recently piled off breach between the weir channel and the lock channel.

Although it could not contribute directly or participate in the Trust's work, the Severn River Board and its officers, particularly L.A. Rhodes, Chief Engineer, and his Deputy L.W. Haines, were always very helpful and co-operative, both with advice and in designing

Pershore Watergate, 1956. The masonry has been removed to water level. Royal Engineers prepare explosive charges for underwater demolition. D.H. Burlingham is in a duffle coat.

their schemes to take account of the Trust's needs. Later the Board's large dragline forded the weir channel and large scale earth works continued until they were completed in early June. *Pisgah* could now resume her journey to Pershore Mill.

The new lock gates were fitted in March and were of very good quality. Made from dimensions taken on site nine months earlier, the gates were a perfect fit and needed no adjustment before the lock was flooded. Following the fitting, presentations were made to Foreman Munn and his men in recognition and gratitude for all their skilled help.

Permission was sought from and readily given by Partridge's to use a short length of bank above and below the lock for landing stages, and to site a small lock-side hut. They also agreed a pedestrian right of access, for nominated Trust personnel, to the lock-side for inspection and maintenance purposes.

When Concrete Piling left the site, the Trust bought from them their foreman's site hut. This hut continued to be used by volunteer lock-keepers until it was destroyed by floods in April 1998.

The clear channel where the old watergate had been, the deepened channel through Pershore Old Bridge, the realigned approach channel and the deepened lock were ceremonially reopened on 8 July by Mrs Bulkeley-Johnson of the Mrs Smith Trust. *Pisgah* was the official craft.

Some mention should be made at this stage about the demise of Pershore Watergate. It was believed to be the last working watergate, certainly in Britain if not in Europe. In the 1950s there was no generally accepted culture of preservation or conservation. The restoration or conservation of a river navigation – in itself considered a most peculiar project – was regarded as a whole, and individual parts might well have to suffer for the sake of the overall scheme. As far as I can recall, the possible conservation of the watergate was never raised, let alone considered; it was an obstruction to efficient navigation and therefore it had to go.

Nafford Lock, 1955. The gate is being lifted out for replanking. Note the single pole lifting tackle.

Today it would probably be a listed structure, needing Listed Building consent for any alterations or repairs. Demolition would be completely unthinkable. Could it have been preserved? Certainly not as a part of the navigable river, for reasons already explained. It might have been theoretically possible to construct a new navigation channel around it, isolating it from the main river channel, and leave it to silt up. The purchase of land required, coupled with the construction work on such a channel, would have presented a prohibitive and totally unacceptable cost to the Trust, and it is unlikely that the Seven River Board would have accepted a realigned channel. Before the demolition a careful photographic record was made, which is in the Worcestershire County Record Office. Similar observations apply to Cropthorne Watergate, which was derelict and unusable when demolished in 1961.

Pershore Lock, 1956. Presentation to Foreman Munn by C.D. Barwell. Mrs Barwell is on the right.

Pershore Watergate, 1955, seen from upstream. The spill weir is on the left. Large lashers (paddles) are open in the centre, and the navigation gate is open. Photo courtesy of Worcestershire County Record Office.

Pershore Watergate, 1955. Note the operating gear for the navigation gate paddles, and the winch with post and snatch blocks for opening/closing the gate. Photo courtesy of Worcestershire County Record Office.

Pershore Lock, 1955, ceremonial reopening. Pisgah *is entering the deepened lock with the official party.*

5 1956 and 1957: odds and ends

In June 1956, the directors of Collins Brothers (Evesham) Ltd, makers of 'Tower Brand' pork pies and sausages, and owners of Evesham Mill and adjoining premises, Evesham Weir, the derelict Evesham Lock, and the sluices with an eel trap and adjacent island, offered, subject to certain conditions, to give the weir, lock, sluice and island to the Trust. The lock, while not part of the Lower Avon Navigation, would give access to the Upper Avon once restored. There was a good deep channel from the lock 3 miles upstream to Norton Corner. While this was a splendid offer which clearly had to be accepted, my report on the property to the Trust's Finance and General Purposes Committee, on the weir in particular, concluded: '…in presenting this to the Trust, the present owners will be relieving themselves of a big liability.' And so it turned out. Immediate repair works were required to fill large scour holes in the weir, which might well have breached if neglected over the winter, and to fill large voids under the crest and toe of the weir.

Despite the success at Pershore, it was important that the Trust did not neglect those parts of the restored Navigation which, while operable, were in poor repair. I produced a report on the condition of the whole Navigation for the Trust Council in October 1956, which recommended replacement of the upstream gates at Avon Lock and both pairs of gates at Nafford as soon as funds allowed.

In August essential improvements were made to the lock-keeper's cottage at Avon Lock, Tewkesbury. Proper sanitation was installed, together with a mains water supply and electricity. The cottage had been dependent on well water, oil lamps and Calor gas lighting, with drainage directly to the river. Both new supplies had to be laid underground from adjacent property, and the relevant wayleaves obtained.

1956 also saw the publication of *Cruising on Shakespeare's Avon*, a thirty page guidebook containing rules, advice and general information with maps of the river. This publication has been revised over the years and is now called *Gateway to the Avon*, currently in its thirteenth edition.

The Trust was now deeply in debt, and great efforts had to be made to raise funds. New legislation – the Lotteries and Gaming Act 1956 – presented an opportunity. General public attitude to gambling at the time was somewhat ambivalent, so the approval of Trust supporters was sought before the introduction of a monthly lottery which raised several hundred pounds. Barwell also devised a basic form of direct mail appeal using Sell's *Directory of roads and streets in Birmingham*, but this method required excessive administrative time to ensure all monies received were properly acknowledged. Appeal letters were also sent to all known private boat owners.

★★★★★

Evesham Weir, 1956. P.H. Protheroe, Hon. Treasurer, is inspecting the large scour hole.

In January 1957, when Pershore Lock with its newly deepened downstream approach channel had been in use for six months, Partridge's the Pershore millers and owners of the main dam and weir, reported that part of the main dam adjacent to the newly deepened channel had slipped by about 2ft. At this point, the dam was only about 20ft wide and was retaining an 8ft 6in head of water. Instability in a man-made earth structure, probably several hundred years old, was very serious, and was probably caused by the deepening of the channel. Who would be liable for the cost of remedial works? Prices were obtained, which the miller did not accept. An impasse seemed likely but action was essential.

Fortunately the Severn River Board had plans for major realignment of both the weir discharge channel, which at that time flowed round a long and tortuous channel called 'the gut', and for their flood control sluice discharge channel. To enable these improved channels to be made, the downstream approach channel to the lock would have to be realigned; this would widen and greatly strengthen the unstable dam. Work began and continued satisfactorily throughout the summer, but the autumn, winter and spring of 1958 brought six major floods, causing extensive damage to the newly formed channels and temporary stoppage of work. During the works, the Navigation had to be closed, severely inconveniencing the miller, although it was temporarily reopened for a few days in April. Work was finally completed at the beginning of July 1958, at a cost to the Severn River Board of £18,200, towards which the Trust contributed £1,350 – a good bargain. The flood control sluice was later enlarged and realigned in 1976 by the Severn Trent Water Authority, then responsible for land drainage, causing no inconvenience to the Navigation.

Back to 1957. As further restoration was completed and with further projects in mind, it was clear that the Trust needed more work boats, for use both as floating work platforms and for transport of equipment and materials to otherwise relatively inaccessible sites. In April two 25ft x 10ft ex-RAF refueller barges, *Chestnut* and *Elm,* were bought by Barwell

The newly acquired and adapted Chestnut *is towed to Wyre Mill, 1957.*

– the Trust needed them but did not have the money. The vessels were brought by road from Scotland to Sharpness Docks, where they were adapted for Trust use: *Chestnut* had a short mast and derrick fitted and both had hatch covers made. They were towed to Tewkesbury by *Pisgah.* Barwell and his wife in *North Star* and R. Burrowes and family in *Daphne II,* with several Trust members as barge crews, then towed the two barges from Tewkesbury to the Trust's wharf at Wyre Mill – sixteen miles. Both vessels were in intermittent use for twenty-four years and proved valuable assets.

During 1957 the long running dispute over the £400 Annuity was finally settled. A payment, largely funded by sums already received and held in a suspense account, was made; all future Annuity income could be used for Trust purposes. The Annuity continues to be paid to the Trust as proprietors of the Lower Avon Navigation.

Deepening Fladbury Lock
Earlier in 1957 Barwell had approached the Pilgrim Trust and the Dulverton Trust for possible grants. At that time the Trust's objectives and works fell outside the remit of the Pilgrim Trust, but the Dulverton Trust showed interest, asking for a specific task to be identified and a rough estimate of likely costs produced. The deepening of Fladbury Lock was chosen as a project and a rough price obtained of £7-8,000. Sadly, in June, the Dulverton Trust turned down the Trust's request. However, an anonymous gift of £2,000 was made in May.

While there were no funds immediately available to deal with either the whole or part of the 'the last 600 yards' between the derelict Cropthorne Watergate and the derelict Fladbury Lock, it was essential for fund-raising that the Trust should decide how this project should be tackled and know in some detail what it would cost. Barwell accordingly convened a discussion group comprising the members of the former PLRC. After resolving in rough outline how the job could be done, they considered that an overall minimum cost of £15,000 was likely.

Then in May, Thomas Vale and Sons Ltd, the civil engineering contractor which had

Fladbury Lock, 1957, deepening the lock floor. Here the floor is partly deepened. Note the horizontal cross timber with material beneath (later removed) in the middle ground, with the top cill behind and a top gate leaning against the top cofferdam (prior to re-planking). Note also the holes in the lock walls, used to support steamers for dry-docking.

restored the lock chamber of Wyre Lock three years previously, made a surprise offer. Vales had no immediate work for their piling gang, and offered a prompt start at Fladbury Lock to deepen it and carry out other specified works for an all inclusive price of £8,850, the Trust to pay when it had the money. Following a special meeting of the Trust Council, this most generous offer was gratefully accepted. The former PLRC was reconstituted as the Fladbury Lock Restoration Committee (FLRC) with me as chairman and the other members as before.

The work required at Fladbury was to deepen the lock chamber and downstream cills by 4ft 6in and effect repairs to walls. Deepening was necessary in anticipation of the removal of the derelict Cropthorne Watergate, the use of which had been necessary to provide a navigation depth over the downstream lock cill. The method adopted was to remove the remains of the timber plank lock floor, temporarily leaving the timber cross beams in situ. Gravel and soil between the beams and beneath the lock walls (supported on horizontal timbers and timber piles) was then removed by grab and hand shovel one section at a time and replaced at a lower level, one section at a time, with reinforced concrete. The horizontal cross beams were removed as the concreted sections were completed, making a U section invert on the floor and underpinning the brick walls. The horizontal timbers were removed section by section. Wall repairs consisted of straightforward brickwork repairs and some reinforced concrete replacement.

It is interesting to note that in the lock walls were eight holes approximately 1ft square,

Fladbury Lock, 1957, deepening the lock floor. Note the sawn off ends of horizontal cross timbers (later to be removed) above the newly excavated floor.

four along each side, opposite each other and approximately 4ft above the lower water level. By inserting large timbers across the lock chamber into these holes, the lock could be used as a dry dock for the periodic hull inspections of the steamers *Gaiety* and *Hurley* from Evesham. When water in the lock was at a lower level, with Cropthorne Watergate open, there would have been no more than 1ft of water covering the lock floor making inspection quite accessible.

No one noticed at the time that the lock walls were very slightly out of vertical, thus producing a tapered lock chamber that was approximately 5in narrower at low water level than it was at top water level.

As excavation work in the lock chamber progressed, a problem of excess water had to be overcome. Beneath the lock was a layer of water-bearing gravel through which flowed a strong underground stream, the capacity of which was far beyond that of the two 6in pumps initially on site. These were diesel-engined pumps which would have had to be kept running all night if the lock was to be dry at start of work time each day, and would therefore require a night watchman to ensure their continued operation. To overcome this problem a sump was dug in the lock bottom on the course of the underground stream, a temporary 440 volt mains electricity supply was brought across the adjacent field to the lock site, and additional electrically driven submersible 6in pumps operated by float switch were installed until the overall pump capacity exceeded that of the underground stream. The pumps were kept running continuously, controlled by the float switch.

The exciting time came at the end of the job when the suction pipes had to be withdrawn without excessive flooding of the completed – apart from the sump – reinforced concrete lock

Fladbury Lock, 1957. Fitting new top cill capping against re-planked top gates.

floor, downstream cill and underpinning. The size of the sump was reduced by shuttered concrete walls, the top of which were about 1ft below the new lock floor, and tied into the new reinforced concrete floor. Into these walls were cast four large strong bolts. A $\frac{1}{4}$in thick steel plate complete with seal was made which could be bolted over the sump hole. The electricity to the pumps was then switched off, the suction pipes were removed very quickly and the steel plate was bolted down to stop ingress of water from the underground stream. All this had to be done in no more than a five minute period. Rapid setting reinforced concrete was then laid over the steel plate, sealing the stream beneath the lock.

The upstream lock gates were in sufficiently good condition to be re-planked. New, deeper, downstream gates would be needed before the lock could be used, but with no money to pay for them, measurements for them were taken so that they could be made and fitted at a later, as yet unknown, date.

Various events: new gates at Nafford

At Nafford Lock a gate anchor strap fractured in August 1957 and had to be replaced. The new strap was made at Barwell's works and fitted two days later by volunteer labour.

Amicable negotiations proceeded with Captain J.F. Bomford to purchase land, derelict buildings and land access to Fladbury Lock. The freehold of the lock sites purchased in 1950 basically consisted of the width and length of the lock chambers, including their stone parapets and land covered by 'the swing of the balance arms.' Additional lock-side land at other sites has been acquired through negotiation over the last fifty years, to provide the areas now used and maintained by the Trust. By August 1958 the purchase of additional land at Fladbury Lock was complete. During the next three months volunteer working parties including R. Lee, R. Sankey Smith, R. Burrowes, H.F. Muston, D.C.B. Mathews, I. Saward, D.H. Clarke, R.F. Muston, B. Scott and A. Smith, erected a concrete post and wire boundary fence, and generally adapted the derelict lock-side building as a store.

In November a 'water boil', a small vertical column of water, was reported coming from the central slope of Nafford Weir. No one accepted any responsibility for the maintenance of this weir, which had been rebuilt on a new site in the 1920s, so if repairs were needed the Trust would have to do them. By arrangement the Severn River Board 'drew' the river at Nafford, thus drying off the weir for inspection by J.L. Sanders and me. As well as the hole through which the water 'boiled', there was considerable scour at both ends of the weir. Apart from tipping some stone to retard the erosion of a scoured bank, other remedial works would have to be delayed until funds were available. However, a close watch needed to be kept on this deteriorating structure. While the water level was down, Foreman Munn took detailed measurements for two new pairs of lock gates, to be made when the cash position allowed.

A further fund-raising event took place in the autumn, unknown to Barwell. Trust members and supporters raised £591 for the 'Douglas Barwell Appreciation Fund' – a gesture which both surprised and delighted him, while adding to Trust funds.

By patching and make-do-and-mend repairs Nafford Lock had been kept functioning for eight years. The time for major repairs was now long overdue. An earlier detailed underwater survey by Barwell had shown '…a lack of solid structures in line with the stank slots, no cross beams, broken timber flooring and much underwater erosion.'

During the summer of 1958, timber for two new pairs of lock gates was ordered and their construction began at Diglis workshops, Worcester. A very wet autumn subsequently made ground conditions difficult. At the beginning of November, *Pisgah* collected the new lock gates from Diglis and delivered them to the lock-side. They were unloaded in pouring rain which continued throughout the following night, causing a flood and postponement of the work by a week. The following week stanks were installed, but such was the appalling condition of the lock floors that dewatering proved very difficult, taking four days and several additional pumps. While Foreman Munn and his men proceeded with cill replacement and gate fitting, Perks Bros, builders of Eckington, carried out wall repairs below the water line and some floor repairs. The very wet and muddy lock-side conditions made work difficult and hazardous. The only lifting device was a single pole derrick with a manually operated winch and block and tackle, which was the method then in use for lifting and handling lock gates on site. The weight of a lock gate – in excess of two tons – plus the weight of the steel pole, making a point load on, or more accurately in, very soft muddy surfaces, caused much difficulty. The way in which Foreman Munn and his men worked was a great tribute to their skill, experience and tenacity.

By early December the job was complete and the lock working. The cost was £1,822, but the Trust's bank account was overdrawn to its agreed limit and the job could wait no longer, so Barwell made a short term interest-free loan to tide over the finances – not for the first or the last time.

Preparing for the final effort – clearing outstanding problems
Regarding 1959, Barwell commented 'Obviously this coming year will need to be one of retrenchment, followed by considerable planning of our final assault.' And so it proved.

In February the Trust was offered, and accepted, a free of charge stand space at the Midland Boat Show, a week long event. The stand was set up and staffed by a rota of

Nafford Lock, 1958. Clearing lock floor before repairs.

volunteers. It provided another occasion for a television interview, adding valuable momentum to the forthcoming 'Last 600 yards' Appeal. The following year the Trust returned to the Show with encouraging results. Founder Council member K. Gill Smith agreed to prepare and have printed an Appeal leaflet which, on its appearance, received widespread approbation. G.R. Speed revived his 1952 'Save the Avon' Appeal Committee.

Sadly in February, E.J. Price, the Trust's Secretary, suffered a heart attack and his work had to be done by others on a temporary basis. His health did not fully recover; he resigned as Secretary at the January 1960 Annual General Meeting, and died a year later. His meticulous administrative abilities, his wide knowledge of the area and its people, together with his calm and, necessarily at times, restraining attitude were of inestimable value to the Trust in its first decade. During 1960 Council Member D.V.S. Cottrell introduced Barwell to Commander R.W. Anstice RN (retd), with a view to him doing administrative tasks for the Trust. He became the Trust Secretary at the January 1961 Annual General Meeting and served with great efficiency and good humour for five years.

Letters from Barwell to various previously supportive charitable trusts produced over £1,000, which all helped to relieve the indebtedness to Vales. Speed's 'Last 600 yards' Appeal organisation was coming together, and an appeal launch was planned for March 1960.

In November an underwater obstruction was reported at Pershore Lock. Diving investigations by Barwell revealed that one of the 10ft long cast iron channel section stank slots was lying on the floor in front of the upper lock gates. Further examination showed that the normal timber stank cill had disappeared. This meant that it would not be possible to install a normal stank with timbers that was safe; the only alternative would be to pile off the lock entrance, entailing costs of £1,250. The position was well summarised by Barwell's terse comment: 'finance does not at present permit us to proceed.' Remedial work had to wait until 1961.

Cropthorne Watergate – Fladbury Lock. 'The last 600 yards' overall plan. Note the six separate sections.

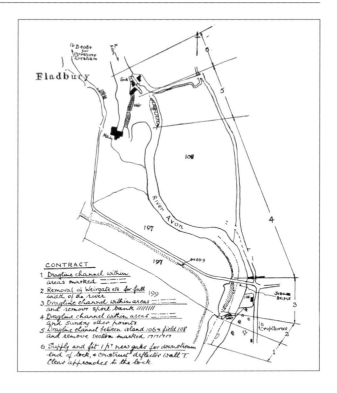

Also in November the FLRC made a detailed survey of the river from just downstream of Cropthorne Watergate right up to Fladbury Lock – the last 600 yards – and they produced an overall plan for the task, which devolved neatly into six sections. Each could stand alone as a separate contract if necessary, to be done as funds allowed. The final stage of the Lower Avon restoration scheme was beginning to take shape.

1960 began with a report of problems at Pershore – both at the lock and at the weir which was owned by the miller. Winter floods, heavy frost and strong winds combined to damage many riverside banks, causing excessive silting in places. One such place was the mouth of Pershore Lock. The extent of the silting was such that the upper gates could not be opened and *Pisgah* was unable to travel the 400 yards from the lock to Pershore Mill. A scour hole was also sighted in the weir.

The silt shoal was removed by Bomford & Wilkins Limited of Binton, using a suction dredger. The job took just under three weeks, and about 70 tons of spoil was pumped to the base of the main dam retaining wall. The weir, not the Trust's responsibility, was kept under regular observation.

'The last 600 yards' Appeal for £8,000 was launched with a national press conference held in Cropthorne Village Hall, attended by national, regional and local press and BBC and ITV television and radio. After the presentation to the press and a question and answer session, the proceedings were adjourned to the last 600 yards of the river nearby for on site inspection and more questions. I explained the technicalities of what had to be done; Speed very effectively explained the ways in which the money would be raised. Articles and pictures later appeared in *The Times, The Daily Telegraph, The Guardian, Warwickshire and Worcestershire, Yachts and Yachting, Motorboat and Yachting, Birmingham Post, Wolverhampton Express and Star, Coventry Evening Telegraph* as well as more local newspapers. Local appeals were planned for the autumn in Evesham, Pershore and Tewkesbury.

In April, P.H. Protheroe retired. He was the manager of the Evesham branch of the National Provincial Bank, the Trust's Treasurer and, since the resignation of Sir R. Kerr, Trust Vice Chairman. With E.J. Price, he had a wide knowledge of the Vale of Evesham and its inhabitants, and his wise, good-humoured counsels were invaluable. From shortly after the Trust's inception, Protheroe was chairman of the Trust's Finance and General Purposes Committee, which used to hold its regular monthly meetings in a back room of the Talbot Inn in Port Street, Evesham; the Talbot was about half way between Protheroe's house and the Bank and a regular place for refreshment for him.

Those attending the monthly meetings would order their drink at the bar before proceeding to the back room. The drinks would then be brought in and distributed; at half-time a list for refills was taken to the bar and again drinks brought to us. My recollection is that Protheroe always had two pints of beer, Barwell whisky and water, Goodall, Cottrell and Sanders beer, Raymer and I rough cider. Anstice, not a teetotaller, inevitably had nothing: 'no one can say they have seen me with a glass in my hand' – it was the early days of drink-driving legislation. These monthly meetings continued at the Talbot until there was a change of landlord. Nearly all the Trust's strategic planning for the whole of the Lower Avon Restoration took place in that back room.

The quarterly and occasional extra Council meetings of the Trust were held in the Evesham Borough Council Chamber in Evesham Town Hall. This was a large, dark and dignified room surrounded by portraits of past mayors and boards listing their names and dates. This venue was symbolic of the support that Trust had, and still receives, from this Authority.

During the summer the Trust bought a second-hand, 30cwt capacity, manually-operated derrick crane with a 40ft long jib. This was delivered in parts to Beecham's boatyard at Tewkesbury and towed to the Trust's maintenance wharf at Wyre by volunteers using *Chestnut* and *Elm* behind cruisers belonging to other volunteers. Over a period of several weeks, volunteers constructed bases for the crane, designed by B.W. Thompson, which was then assembled and erected by Foreman Munn and his team. The crane was then subjected to statutory testing requirements and passed as safe for use.

In September one of the upstream lock gates at Avon Lock, Tewkesbury collapsed, forcing a closure of the lock. These top gates were in poor condition well before the Trust's time, and had been patched in 1952. Foreman Munn took measurements for a new pair of gates, but his commitments on the Severn meant that it would be late February or early March 1961 before Avon Lock could reopen. It so happened that Gloucestershire County Council was about to start on the road widening of King John's Bridge near the lock and had negotiated a winter closure of the Navigation at this point. The enforced closure at Avon Lock meant that the Trust was able to allow the Navigation closure at the Bridge to be brought forward by several weeks.

In November Barwell discussed the possible replacement of the wooden lock cottage at

Pershore Lock, 1959. Cast iron stank slot recovered together with brickwork attached. From left to right, D.C.B Mathews, C.D. Barwell in diving suit, T.R. Burrowes.

Pershore Lock, 1960. Shoal being removed by suction dredger.

Avon Lock, Tewkesbury, September 1960. The top lock gates have failed. Note the broken heel post, lying on its side, of the opposite gate, lying on its side, in the right foreground. New replacement gates were installed in April 1961.

Avon Lock with Tewkesbury Borough Council. The timbers were starting to decay, and the brick piers on which the building rested were always damp, being frequently covered by flood water, and consequently were severely frost damaged. The principle of a dwelling constructed on a platform raised above flood level was accepted. October saw the local launchings of the 'Last 600 yards' Appeal in Evesham, Pershore and Tewkesbury, at well-supported public meetings.

While the overall appeal was for £8,000, the Trust knew and made clear that the eventual cost was likely to be very much more (in the event it was £12,800). Evesham and Tewkesbury each pledged to raise £2,000, and Pershore £1,000. The meeting at Evesham was presided over by the Mayor, Lt-Col. R.G. Burlingham, a first subscriber to the Memorandum and Articles, the meeting at Pershore by W.F. Swift of Fladbury, a local land owner who was very supportive over land access rights to Fladbury Lock, and the Tewkesbuy meeting by the Mayor, Cllr H.O. Workman. For the Trust, Speed, Barwell, Goodall and I presented different aspects of the final task. Worcestershire County Council also made a modest – and its first – grant of £200. The fact that after ten years they had acknowledged the work of the Trust as being beneficial was of far greater significance than the amount.

P.H. Protheroe's successor at the National Provincial Bank, W.F. Tunna, was appointed Trust treasurer. One of his first acts was to increase the Trust's overdraft facilities from £1,000 to £3,000, with an emergency reserve overdraft increase from £1,000 to £1,500. While these overdrafts were underwritten by Barwell and W.F. Allen, the fact that they were increased so greatly reflected the financial credibility of the Trust and its past prudent management.

6 The last 600 yards; problems at Pershore

1961 had to be the year of the final effort – not that anything to do with a river is ever final. But looking back, it seemed to be a year when everything happened everywhere at almost the same time.

One of the first things to happen was the formal reconstitution of the FLRC as 'the Works Committee' – the same people but with a much broader brief – to cope with all works of restoration, repair and routine maintenance.

Negotiations for riparian access for 'the last 600 yards' were started early in the year. There was a need for river bank dragline access, sites for dumping considerable volumes of spoil, and access from river bank to those sites. As requirements varied, so did the complexity of the negotiations. It had always been the Trust's policy to offer compensation to riparian owners for access at valuation; usually negotiations could be concluded by settling for replacement or widened field access gates, and/or culverts as required rather than for cash; often access was given freely on condition that sites were 'made good' on completion of works. The Trust has good reason to be grateful to many riparian owners over many years.

In January the Trust's concern over the deteriorating condition of Pershore Weir was reported to the owners, Partridge's of Pershore Mill. A large part of the slope of the weir had washed away, as had one end of the far bank. Partridge's confirmed their intention to employ contractors to make a lasting repair as soon as water levels and general weather conditions allowed.

At Avon Lock, Tewkesbury, the new top gates were ready for fitting. *Pisgah* collected the gates from Diglis workshops and they were installed by Foreman Munn and his team over two weekends in April. The river was then open again for navigation upstream as far as Cropthorne Watergate.

By about this time the various final appeals for funds were well under way, and producing very encouraging results. Appeal organiser G.R. Speed commented:

> The machinery is well and truly established. There are eight committees and sub-committees at work, with seventy-five to a hundred members actively engaged and a major step forward has been achieved with funds. Never in my life have I experienced such an extra ordinary acclamation by all the people from Evesham, Pershore and Tewkesbury who are showing their approval of the Trust's eleven years' work by showing their willingness to help in any way they can.

Quotations were sought and received for the six sections of the last 600 yards. The overall requirement was for a 6ft deep channel from and including the site of Cropthorne

Cropthorne Watergate, 1961, seen from Jubilee Bridge, Fladbury. Note the derelict lashers on the left, the spill weir in the centre, the navigation gate on the right and the very heavy silting. The tree on the right is in the centre of the former navigation channel.

watergate right up to Fladbury Lock. Volunteer workers removed part of the overspill weir of the water gate, loading the stone into work boats to be taken to the Trust's maintenance wharf at Wyre Mill. The section of work immediately upstream of the Watergate, including underneath Jubilee Bridge, was let to Bomford and Wilkins Ltd of Binton. This section was awkward because not only did it include removing the remains of the ford which predated the first Jubilee Bridge, and the pier foundations of that bridge, but it also included shoal and silt removal from beneath the bridge, involving use of a snatch block and tackle on the far bank. There was sufficient low-lying space on the west bank to accommodate all the spoil removed from this area.

Two quotations were considered for the removal of the watergate: from Thomas Vale & Son Ltd of Stourport for £10,000, and from A.E. Farr Ltd of Westbury, Wiltshire for £2,000, with the qualification that if the work could be done for less any saving would be shared on a 50% basis between them and the Trust; if costs exceeded £2,000, additional work would be charged at cost only. They were confident – correctly as it turned out – that the costs would be well within £2,000. Day work sheets detailing labour and plant costs would be submitted to the Trust, so that savings and overruns could be checked. Since I lived within half a mile of the site, I was able to inspect the works almost daily, and the checking of day work sheets was a relatively simple task. Sorry as the Trust was to part with

Cropthorne Watergate, 1961. Demolished material being loaded into Elm *for transport to Pershore Weir.*

Vales, who had always offered most generous terms, £8,000 was a very substantial difference, so Farrs' quotation was accepted. Farrs were in the process of completing a large contract, building the M50 motorway bridge over the river Severn at Queenhill, together with some miles of motorway; they were anxious to keep a nucleus of their skilled staff and plant in the area until another suitable contract came their way. By mid-July they were on site at Cropthorne, rapidly and without fuss breaking up the very substantial structure of the old watergate.

By this time, six months had elapsed since Partridge's expressed their intention to carry out repairs to Pershore Weir. Nothing appeared to have been done and deterioration of the structure continued. On hearing that Cropthorne Watergate was being demolished, Partridge's asked if materials could be loaded into *Pisgah* and used for weir repairs. The Trust readily agreed, and *Pisgah,* together with the Trust's work boats *Chestnut* and *Elm,* breasted up and made the journey to the watergate site and back to Pershore loaded, proving the existence of a deep wide channel to that point. There were problems – Partridge's – in unloading and placing the stone, and weir deterioration continued.

While responsibility for the weir repair was Partridge's and not that of the Trust, the consequences, especially at this time, of any breach, of which there was a very real risk, would be almost catastrophic for the Trust. On the point of a successful conclusion to an eleven year struggle, to have a major breakdown midway along the river would not only cause physical damage to the project, but the effect on the morale of all those involved would be disastrous, as would the effect on the general public who were being asked for

Cropthorne Watergate, 1961. In the foreground, the removal of heavy silting between the watergate and Jubilee Bridge; in the background, the removal of the watergate is in progress.

support. The effect of a breach on the business of Pershore Mill would be far less disastrous. They would not be able to get 30 ton loads of grain directly to the mill – but with so many recent stoppages for the deepening of Pershore Lock and its associated works, that was nothing new, just an awkward inconvenience. There would be loss of water power, but there were plenty of other alternatives for that. So who would make the first move: Partridge's or the Trust?

Back at 'the last 600 yards', work proceeded steadily with the watergate removal, which was completed within three weeks of commencement. So pleased was the Trust with Farr's work that their prices for other sections of the overall job, submitted on the same basis as the watergate removal tender, were readily accepted.

Sections upstream from Jubilee Bridge included some 450 yards of draglining, carting and dumping spoil; reshaping the island downstream of the lock to form an approach channel between the meadow and the island, which also involved carting and dumping spoil; construction of a stone deflector wall between the lock and the island to deflect the weir discharge from the lock approach channel; and piling the field side approach bank below the lock to stabilise it and to enable an adequate depth of water to be achieved. At the same time this would make a very superior (by the standards of 1961!) landing stage.

Immediately upstream from Jubilee Bridge there was about 150 yards of very heavy lias clay on the riverbed on the east side of the river. So impervious was this clay that much of it was dug dry – a temporary bank of this clay from excavated material was placed on the outer edge of the clay deposit roughly along the centre line of the river.

Fladbury, 1961. Channel clearance upstream of Jubilee Bridge. Behind the dragline the heavy marl removal can be seen. Cropthorne Mill and Fladbury Lock are in the background.

Between this temporary embankment and the river bank the very hard clay was broken out a bit at a time. Much of this material was dumped in the area now used as a visitor car park, and the remainder was graded between the river and the access track, and beyond the track. The heavy nature of the material can be readily seen by probing about in the currently overgrown area of the river bank.

Between this clay area and the island below Fladbury Lock there was occasional shoaling with alluvial gravel and mud. This was very easily removed, although it necessitated working from both sides of the river.

Construction of the stone deflector wall between the lock and the island was an awkward if straightforward task. The stones, with an average weight of 4cwt, and the heaviest weighing about half a ton, came from a Forest of Dean quarry. Each stone had to be placed individually and for this purpose two temporary stagings had to be constructed over what is now the approach channel. From the staging a 22RB crane with stone dogs could pick up the stones from the bank and lower them to the position required. Three half-piles were set vertically in the completed wall to act as markers at times of high water; they are also an indication that the wall remains stable in spite of constant water scour from the weir discharge.

Piling the east bank was straightforward, with back walings and anchor piles positioned as appropriate. The bank behind the piles was graded, with a narrow concrete strip being laid for landing. The 'hollows' in the pile sections were timber fendered, with some timbers being raised as mooring posts. These timbers have now decayed and have not been replaced.

The river bed between the lock entrance and the south end of the island was good quality fine gravel, which being wet, 'ran' as it was removed, so more sand and gravel ran in to take its place. Where the bank was piled immediately below the lock, the piles

Fladbury Lock Deflector Wall, 1961. 22RB crane on temporary platform placing stone.

Fladbury Lock Deflector Wall, 1961. Stone being placed.

Fladbury Lock, 1961. Pile driving the east bank below the lock. The pile hammer can be seen on the extreme right, the completed deflector wall is on the left.

retained the sand and the channel could be deepened easily to about 5ft. In the channel between the island and the meadow it was not so easy, and a mean stable depth of 4ft 6in was established – attempts to deepen this area caused bank collapse. The gravel was carted and tipped onto the access track behind the large meadow, greatly improving the track. When the meadow owner, whose permission had been obtained for access, discovered that gravel from his river bed (the approach channel between the island and the meadow) was being tipped onto an access track which he did not own, he objected strongly and required all further materials to be tipped at the far end of his meadow by the meadow entrance gate.

Work on these various sections followed a natural pattern, working upstream. By the end of September the works were substantially complete, with only the new downstream lock gates to be made and fitted at Fladbury Lock. Weather during this time was ideal: dry, warm and sunny. Dredged materials dried out relatively quickly, enabling them to be moved earlier than otherwise.

It was both a pleasure and an education to work with Farrs' team: skilled, experienced, and superbly equipped with modern, well-maintained plant and well backed by a strong support staff – essential for a major civil engineering contract. The Trust was able to enjoy those benefits for its relatively minor works. If adjustments to works were needed, I only had to say and men and plant would appear and the job would be done. Of course, any adjustments were fully detailed on subsequent day work sheets!

Fladbury Lock, 1961. Clearing the downstream approach channel.

Pershore Weir and other jobs

In early September there was still no progress on Pershore Weir repairs. At Barwell's instigation, Sanders, who knew the Partridge brothers quite well, approached them with two suggestions. The first was that with works on 'the last 600 yards' almost complete, the Trust had available nearby an experienced contractor with plant and equipment, and could therefore do all the necessary work very promptly, with the costs to be subsequently apportioned between Partridge's and the Trust. The second suggestion was that Partridge's should sell to the Trust the weir, the main dam between the weir and the lock, the island between the weir discharge channel and the lock approach channel, and that part of the west lock-side adjacent to the mill pond, for a nominal sum. The Trust would then be responsible for all future repairs and maintenance, thereby relieving the miller of a very considerable liability. If either of these suggestions were to be implemented, agreement of the Trust Council would be required. To everyone's surprise Partridge's promptly accepted the second suggestion as a basis for negotiation. Permission was given for immediate access to site for contractors; special meetings of the Trust's Finance and General Purposes Committee and the Trust Council were held, which authorized the legal agreements being drawn up by solicitors for the respective parties. Instructions were given to the Works Committee to proceed urgently with repairs to the weir.

It was now nearly the end of September and only a few more weeks of relatively settled weather could be expected. Deterioration of the weir was rapidly nearing crisis point. Because the Trust had been closely monitoring the condition of the weir, what had to be done was fairly clear, as was the fact that immediate action was necessary.

The major problem was site access. Many lorry loads of large stone would have to be

Pershore Weir, 1961. The east end of the weir is badly scoured. The people on the bank show the scale of the damage.

brought to site and placed. Negotiations were rapidly and successfully concluded with the owner of the meadows adjacent to the weir; field gateways had to be widened, culverts rebuilt and stone laid in some gateways. Discussions with A.E. Farr Ltd indicated rough costs of £5-6,000 which, after the costs (not completely covered by recent appeals) of 'the last 600 yards', were too high to be acceptable. How could they be reduced? Negotiations with the ever helpful Severn River Board and with Partridge's, who controlled the water levels between Pershore and Wyre, enabled water levels both upstream and downstream of the weir to be temporarily substantially lowered. Lower water levels meant a dry weir with no water flowing over it, which considerably aided the placing and tipping of stone. A likely cost saving of £1,000-£2,000 could be achieved. Protective tracking could be laid on the weir face to enable vehicles to reverse with their loads of stone almost to the point where it was needed. Other heavy plant could readily ford the now shallow river bed. Closer inspection of the dry weir revealed other areas of potential weakness which would have to be addressed.

On 3 October the first loads of stone were placed; a week later over 400 tons had been laid. The large and enlarging scour hole was filled and capped, the severely scoured east bank had been filled and revetted with large stone, the full length of the weir toe was strengthened with tipped stone to prevent undertoe erosion, as were various deep areas along the front of the weir crest, which was also repaired. The weir was now secure, subject to regular maintenance.

Advantage was also taken of the lowered water levels to effect essential repairs to the upstream adit walls of Pershore Lock. This particular part of the lock structure had not been involved in the lock deepening six years earlier. One of the cast iron channel section

Pershore Weir, 1961. The scoured area has been partially filled with stone. In the foreground are D.H. Burlingham in a raincoat, and J. Sanders with a pipe.

Pershore Weir, 1961. The extent of the stone tipped along the toe can be seen. The 22RB crane is on the west end of the weir.

Pershore Lock, 1961. Repairs are being made to the top adit walls and top gates. The river level has been drained right down, and in the left foreground are the remains of old timber facing plants to the bank.

stank slots had come away and been recovered by Barwell, diving in November 1959, and it was known that the floor area between the adit walls was so damaged that a safe stank could not be made. The lowered water level now revealed all this and enabled proper repairs to be done in the dry by Foreman Munn and his team. Repairs were also necessary to the upstream lock gates and these were carried out. The under water condition of the main dam between the lock and weir could also be inspected; not surprisingly there was considerable erosion; only tree roots were holding the structure together.

While Farrs were still locally based they had quoted for a new downstream landing stage for Pershore Lock. The new downstream approach channel had high 'battered' (sloped) earth (and therefore muddy) banks, making alongside access almost impossible. A landing stage at this site was not only desirable but essential.

At this stage a general mention of landing stages for locks might be appropriate. In 1950 there were none; vessels landed a crew member to work the locks on the nearest convenient river bank or alternatively on the adit walls if accessible. When appropriate works were carried out at locks, simple landing platforms were incorporated. The need for improved access for boat crews to locks was recognised, but was not considered a spending priority until after the restoration.

The proposed landing stage at Pershore had to be '*Pisgah* proof' – a glancing touch from a floating mass of almost 50 tons would seriously damage anything that was not extremely robust. The basic design was for a steel platform, eventually 60ft long, on piles driven well below the bed of the channel. The piles were pitched both in line and square with the channel to provide maximum rigidity. Work access to the site was to be entirely by water. Farrs' first quotation was unacceptably high, but by reducing the overall size of the stage and by

Pershore Lock, 1961. The lower landing stage is under construction. Note the in line and square setting of the piles, and the pile hammer suspended from the derrick.

providing waterborne transport, a price of £450 was agreed. *Chestnut* and *Elm* were breasted up with special tie beams; an air compressor to drive a pile-driving hammer was loaded on to *Elm*; the derrick on *Chestnut* was used for lifting, pitching and driving the piles. Materials were spread between both boats. This all provided a very stable and versatile working rig.

The whole job, done during October, produced a very sturdy landing stage about two-thirds of the way up the approach channel. A small gangway linked the new stage with the bank, along which a footpath to the lock-side soon became established. Additional staging was added in 1969 to provide a stable waiting area for additional craft and a pleasant, albeit isolated, overnight mooring.

In mid-June 1961 problems were reported at Chadbury Lock, where it appeared that the downstream cills had been displaced. It was not possible to make a proper seal between the cill and the gates. With resources, both financial and personnel, fully committed to 'the last 600 yards' and impending problems at Pershore Weir, the lock had to be formally closed until diminution of other pressures allowed remedial work to be done. This was not so serious, as there was very little traffic in the still isolated Evesham to Fladbury reaches. On completion of repair works at Pershore Lock, Foreman Munn and his team, working at weekends, moved to Chadbury in mid-October. The lock was stanked off and dewatered, but the cause of the problem was never determined. The downstream cills were refixed with longer securing bolts by the end of October, and the lock reopened.

All in all it was quite a busy and satisfactory autumn for the Trust's Works Committee.

7 Triumph

As October 1961 progressed, it looked as though the whole Navigation might be usable from Tewkesbury to Evesham by midsummer 1962; only new downstream lock gates for Fladbury Lock and a lot of tidying up remained to be done.

A decision could now be made to hold a formal reopening of the Navigation in 1962.

At a meeting of the Trust Council held on 17 November, the following resolutions were passed:

1. That the official opening of the Navigation should take place during the Whitsun weekend of 9 and 10 June 1962.

2. That an outline scheme for the reopening of the river be accepted as follows:- the ceremony to cover Saturday and Sunday 9 and 10 June 1962, starting at Tewkesbury and ending at Evesham, and including the conveyance of public representatives from the former to the latter together with Council members, and also including a Service of Thanksgiving in Pershore Abbey on the evening of Saturday 9 and the opening of Fladbury Lock on Sunday 10.

3. That Mrs Barwell be invited to perform the opening ceremony at Fladbury Lock.

The early part of 1962 saw the completion of various relatively small but important tasks. The derelict, open-fronted, brick-built cart shed at Fladbury lock-side, recently acquired, was re-roofed and a timber front installed by the regular volunteer band of Burrowes, Harrison, father and son, Mathews and others, to enable it to be used as day accommodation for weekend volunteer lock-keepers. An exhibition stand was prepared and manned at the Birmingham Boat Show. The legal Conveyance for the purchase of Pershore Weir, main dam and island adjacent to the lock was signed in April.

During the early part of March, negotiations were completed for the purchase of another work boat. This vessel, 54ft x 12ft, was an ex-British Sugar Corporation barge, originally used for moving sugar beet from fenland farms to the sugar beet factory (now demolished) at Ely, Cambridgeshire. During March the vessel was moved by road to Sharpness Docks, where it was modified with a ramp and a strengthened hold bottom to enable it to transport medium-sized plant to those Trust sites which had no or poor land access. The vessel was named *Lantern*, and is now fitted with a hydraulic SKB Kraner arm and is in frequent use. *Lantern's* first task for the Trust was to collect the new bottom lock gates from Diglis Workshop and take them to Fladbury, where they were installed in May, thus completing the very last link of the Trust's prime object 'to restore…the Navigation.'

Fladbury Lock, 1962. The last remaining job of the restoration – installing new bottom gates.

In 1993 values, using the published Retail Price Index (see Appendix E), overall expenditure on the restoration was the equivalent of just over £600,000. Well over half a million pounds raised from public subscription and donations – and spent in twelve years. Quite an achievement.

Detailed planning for the official opening ceremonies continued through March, April and May, and the day for the great occasion duly arrived.

An official 'armada' of eleven craft assembled at Tewkesbury on Saturday 9 June, including Barwell's new cruiser *Aviona*. On board this fleet were those people who had been closely involved in various different ways with the restoration project; those who did not have boats were assembled on Beecham's large tripping vessel *Commodore*. Each vessel had its allotted place in the procession and its designated mooring position while waiting at locks. The armada proceeded upstream to Pershore, where it was formally received by the Chairman of Pershore Rural District Council and by Chairmen of riparian Parish Councils. A Thanksgiving Service was held in Pershore Abbey, at which a plain lock key was presented as a symbolic offering of thanks. The lock key can be seen in the Abbey on the west wall, south of the west door.

A large team of volunteer lock-keepers, led by Mathews, very efficiently assisted the rapid passage of the armada through all the locks so that the procession of craft was not unduly disrupted.

The whole event was planned with great precision, and worked extremely well. There was, however, one complication which not many of those taking part were aware of at the time.

10 June 1962. Mrs Betty Barwell cuts the ribbon on the site of the demolished Cropthorne Watergate, formally reopening the Navigation of the Lower River Avon.

The official boat procession was led by two full-length narrow boats: founder Council member C.H. Taplin's *Primrose* and A. Lehmann's *Snail*. These ex-working, wooden hulled narrow boats, 72ft long by 6ft 10in beam (width), were luxuriously converted with cabins, saloons and all mod cons. *Snail* even had an upright piano on board. Such boats were virtually unknown on the river at that time. As working boats, both had expanded in their beams; not uncommon in this type of craft.

Having the two narrow boats breasted up together side-by-side was a new experience for anyone unfamiliar with broad canal usage, and probably a first on the Avon; it was certainly a first for full-length narrow boats. They led because they were the slowest craft; all others had to keep astern of them.

The width and length of Lower Avon locks varies slightly. All went well until the two narrow boats reached Fladbury Lock, which, as related in Chapter 5, has tapered sides. Here the boats stuck and had to be locked through singly, causing a slight delay. Further problems arose at Chadbury Lock, where the length of the lock chamber between bottom gates and top cill was too short (see Chapter 3) and the two boats sadly had to drop out of the procession. The procession was not rehearsed, and this problem could probably not have been foreseen.

On Sunday 10 June, the armada proceeded to the site of Cropthorne Watergate where a white ribbon stretched across the river was ceremonially cut by Mrs Barwell on board *Aviona*, thus formally reopening the Lower Avon Navigation from Evesham to the sea. At

10 June 1962, Fladbury Lock. Commemorative plaque unveiled by LANT council member K. Gill Smith.

Fladbury Lock everyone disembarked for a buffet luncheon, during which Barwell was presented with a binnacle for *Aviona* by his friends and supporters, a gift which was personal to him and which he could not convert, as with previous gifts, to the Trust's benefit. Trust Council Member K. Gill Smith unveiled a commemorative plaque by the lock-side, a facsimile of which may be seen there today. The armada continued to Evesham, where it was formally welcomed and received on the Workman Gardens by the Mayor of Evesham. For those attending it was a memorable climax to twelve years of hard work, and for those working the locks and helping with the smooth running of the event it was a splendid job well done.

The end of the beginning was achieved.

Part III Development
8 Byelaws

After that wonderful, euphoric Whit weekend what was next? The Trust's first purpose – 'to restore' – had been achieved, but its other objectives 'to maintain and improve…' remained.

Preliminary steps had already been taken to address the most important long-term problem of maintaining and improving the Trust's level of income; the new attitude of many charitable organisations, which had been very generous in their past support, was that the prime object – restoration – had been achieved, and that the problem of maintaining that which had been restored was now the Trust's. There were plenty of other good causes equally deserving of their support; the great wide world did not owe the Trust a living; get on with it! Not every boat on the Avon used the locks, and of those which did, not everyone paid every time. True, there were over eight hundred individual members of the Trust, but with a minimum annual membership subscription of half a guinea or ten shillings and sixpence, even with most members paying considerably more, there would be a very big shortfall.

The long term financing of the Trust was a very real problem, the answer to which would either ensure the Trust's financial stability and thereby its continuance, or in the event that a lasting solution could not be found, its demise.

While the solution took over ten years to resolve, its story is probably best told as a single narrative at this stage, rather than in instalments scattered over the years ahead.

Back in 1960, when it was clear that the end of the restoration of the Navigation was in sight, Barwell discussed the problem with Council member D.V.S. Cottrell, who was a solicitor. Subsequently a Bye-laws Committee was set up with Cottrell as chairman, which initially made a careful study of bye-laws used by existing Navigations. Together with the Trust's solicitor, C. Beale, and Mr E.W. Christie of Council, draft bye-laws were prepared, agreed by the Trust Council and submitted to the Ministry of Transport. The Ministry challenged the Trust's legal rights shown by Mr Christie's Council's Opinion and the carefully considered draft bye-laws and Registration Scheme were turned down flat after five years of quite intensive work. The Trust had no funds at that time for a potentially expensive legal battle, but there was no intention of letting the matter drop.

In 1965, a disaster happened at Barmouth, involving a boat, the *Dalwynne*, causing considerable loss of life. The inquest found that there were no bye-laws on the river to ensure adequate and sufficient safety apparatus on boats. This finding provoked a letter from the Ministry of Transport to all Navigation Authorities stating that in future all river Navigations should be regulated by bye-laws. The letter had the gall to ask the Trust what action it proposed. The Trust answered that bye-laws had already been submitted to the Ministry, that they had replied that the Trust had no right to bye-laws and its submission had been refused! The Ministry then asked that the draft bye-laws should be resubmitted and said that they would reconsider the legal position. In October 1967, Cottrell, Beale and Mr Christie went to meet the Ministry in London and negotiate with their lawyers; the draft was approved, and the opinion expressed that the Trust's seventeenth-century Order in Council was in fact a legal title. The first of many hurdles was overcome; the Ministry and Trust were on the same side.

The bye-laws themselves were the easy part; the legal framework by which they could achieve authority was more complex, which meant more delays. Various legal possibilities were considered, the best being an amendment to the 1968 Transport Bill by the House of Lords. In due time an amendment was made to allow the Minister of Transport to authorize private waterways to make bye-laws. This amendment became Section 113 of the Act.

Draft bye-laws were published for public consultation; objections were considered by the Bye-laws Committee, the Trust's legal adviser and the Ministry, and were satisfactorily resolved.

In broad outline the bye-laws required certain safety precautions be taken by vessels, that they carry certain safety equipment, that they be used in a safe and responsible manner, and that all craft on the river be registered annually by the Trust for a fee. All registered craft would be allowed to use the locks on the river without further charge.

The Worcestershire County Council Act of 1968 cancelled a right under the 1751 River Avon Act for riparian owners to use the river free of all charges irrespective of the size of vessel. This right was now restricted to unpowered vessels of under 15ft in length.

The Minister of Transport finally approved the bye-laws in August 1972. The Trust Chairman's Statement for that year said '...the bye-laws give the Trust, as Navigation Authority, regulations whereby a degree of control can be exercised over the use of the river, principally by simple safety requirements, and the compulsory registration of all craft. The number of people using the river for all purposes – cruising, sailing, angling, rowing, canoeing, swimming, picnicking on the bank, or just being by the river, is growing at an enormous rate – and the size of the river itself cannot grow. More and more activity therefore has to be accommodated in the same space. It is hoped that the new bye-laws will better enable all to enjoy the river without disturbance of other interests.'

The granting of bye-laws, to which minor revisions were made in 1992, was, and is, probably the most important event in the existence of the Trust, after that of the restoration itself.

While the Trust now – in 1972 – had powers to require all craft to be registered at an appropriate charge, such charges could not be more than the boat owners would be willing – under the new duress – to pay. A simple calculation soon revealed that the Trust could end up with a shortfall of roughly £5,000 each year, equal to the income from about 100 boats of average size. How could the boat population be increased on an already crowded river?

Cottrell and W.J. Beecham, a Tewkesbury boat builder, Trust Council member and original subscriber to the Trust's Articles, consulted together. Behind his Tewkesbury moorings Beecham had several acres of unused land which could be developed as a marina basin, and Cottrell had a Development Company which could provide the required capital. Shortly after these initial negotiations, Beecham was tragically killed, and the Trust lost an active and very supportive Council member. Negotiations continued with Beecham's company and by the end of 1971 the first sixty berths at the new marina were in use, followed by a further sixty-five berths in 1972. So the shortfall in boat population was made up and the Trust's immediate financial problems resolved. The marina now has three hundred and fifty berths and provides about one third of the Trust's registration income.

9 Evesham Lock restoration

Back now to the time immediately after the reopening of the Navigation. There was much to be done. The overall state of the Trust's installations still included a number of weak spots, in particular the condition of the top gates at Wyre Lock. These were re-planked during the 1954 restoration, and would not hold together for much longer, especially with the increased river use of the now fully restored Lower Avon. An order was placed for new gates, which were installed by Foreman Munn and his team in 1963.

Beyond the Avon, encouraged by the success of the Trust, the IWA-inspired restoration of the southern section of the Stratford-upon-Avon Canal was proceeding rapidly. HM The Queen Mother graciously reopened the canal in July 1964. Already those looking in the longer term at the inland waterways scene were contemplating completion of the link between Evesham and Stratford-upon-Avon, through the restoration of the abandoned and completely derelict Upper Avon Navigation. At Evesham, the Trust owned the derelict Evesham Lock, upstream of which was two and a half miles of navigable Upper Avon.

Among those looking at all aspects of an Upper Avon restoration was Barwell; he was under some pressure to extend his commitments by taking a more active part in planning its restoration. Business commitments, and continued involvement in the Lower Avon (the strain of the past hectic and stressful twelve years later caused a temporary enforced absence on medical advice) made him wary of yet more involvement. However, there was still Evesham Lock…

Shortly after the successful events of Whit weekend 1963, approaches were made to Barwell with various offers of funds to proceed with the prompt restoration of Evesham Lock. The Trust was not in a position to accept these offers, as it had agreed to settle its outstanding debts to A.E. Farr Ltd for the 'last 600 yards' and the unplanned work at Pershore Weir before undertaking any future major works. However, an offer was made that could not be lightly refused. Special meetings of the Trust's Finance and General Purposes Committee and Council were held which authorised acceptance of this generous offer, subject to Farrs' agreement to the new circumstances of their debtor, the Trust. The Trust Council also invited me 'to take overall control of the project,' which I accepted.

When Farrs were approached regarding the Trust's new proposed project, they responded not only by releasing the Trust from its commitment not to start major new works before paying off its debts, but also by offering to do the restoration works on generous and acceptable terms. The Trust was extremely fortunate in having – again – the services of such an experienced contractor for such a comparatively small (for them) job.

Evesham Lock was believed to have been last used in the mid-1920s by the barge collecting tar from Evesham Gas Works, and since acquired by the Trust in 1956 it had been completely derelict. The upstream gates were completely silted up; the gate planking had so deteriorated that in 1960 timber piles faced with galvanised corrugated sheets were driven into the silt in front of the gates to maintain the water level upstream of the weir. Part of one downstream lock gate was in situ; the other gate had disappeared. The lock chamber, constructed of local lias stone, was in fair condition – probably because of the cover provided by the large mature chestnut trees growing on either side of the lock.

In 1962, knowing that 'something' might happen in the relatively near future, a close preliminary examination was made of the methods which would have to be used for the restoration.

There were two separate tasks – interdependent and both having the same major snag – extreme difficulty of access. The first task was comparatively straightforward: the lock had to be piled off from the river and dewatered, such repairs and reconstructions as were then found to be necessary had to be done, and two new pairs of lock gates had to be made and fitted. The second task was not so simple: the downstream river approaches to the lock had completely silted up, and no proper navigation channel existed between the Workman Bridge and Evesham Rowing Club Boathouse, a quarter of a mile downstream. A new channel had to be excavated, and because of the Abbey Park and Workman Gardens on either side of the river there could be no land access; the whole channel-digging work had to be water-borne. This meant that a digging machine (A Priestman 'Wolf' with grab) had to be mounted on a pontoon, secured and moved by cables attached to mature trees in the park and gardens, the trunks of which had to be protected. All the spoil dug – estimated to be 1500 cubic yards – had to be carried by barge to an unloading point, unloaded, and then carted to tip. Such triple handling was very expensive.

The lock access problem was that a 3ft width and 5cwt maximum load limit was the only route to the lock-side. Temporary bridges capable of taking a 10ft width and a 15 ton load were made to enable heavy plant to be taken to the lock-side and the area where spoil was to be unloaded and tipped. A 20ft slipway was also made to enable a large sectional pontoon, from which the digging machine worked, to be assembled and launched. All this involved at least a month's hard work before the job itself could be started.

The lock was eventually piled off, pumped dry, cleared out and examined. The condition of the walls was comparatively good. The floors were bad – non-existent in places – and cills had to be renewed and the quoins remade in concrete. No stank slots or cills existed and, as was the Trust's practice on every lock restoration, these were incorporated in the structure.

Timber for the new gates was delivered to the Diglis workshop at Worcester, where Foreman Munn made two pairs of gates. When finished in May, the gates were loaded on to the Trust's *Lantern* and towed right into the lock at Evesham for installation.

The channel excavation job proved to be more difficult than was originally envisaged. When the Workman Gardens and Abbey Park river frontages were laid out in 1856, a number of small islands and wharf frontages were removed to make the long clear water vista up to the Workman Bridge. The Trust's requirement was a channel in the centre of the river approximately 30ft wide and 5ft deep. But instead of soft, silted mud, there were deposits of hard-packed alluvial gravel and in parts quite large stones. This meant that digging was very slow. The size and weight, and consequently the amount of 'bite', of the

Tewkesbury c.1920. Sluice (removed in 1963) showing the footbridge over with diamond lattice guard rails
The footbridge is now part of the lower landing stage at Evesham Lock. Avon Lock cottage is in the background.

equipment was limited by what was safe to use on the pontoon. However, as the weeks passed, the pontoon and grab gradually dug their way downstream from the lock leaving beneath them a channel of the specified size.

Spoil was carried by barge to Evesham main island, where a second Priestman 'Wolf' unloaded it. Dumpers, and later a tractor shovel, then carried it down the island where it was spread and levelled. The average height of at least half the island is now greater by about 3ft then previously, which makes that part free from normal winter flooding.

Ancillary works included the driving of two steel marker piles to indicate the edge of the dredged channel below the lock, the erection of a substantial (for 1963) steel downstream landing stage, and the excavation and clearance of two mill sluices. Now only one marker pile is evident; the second has been engulfed by the extension of a silt spit which now supports a growth of willow trees and nettles. The original landing stage was once a footbridge over a sluice at Tewkesbury, which the Severn River Board was about to demolish. The Trust bought it for £50, and it was carried to site on *Lantern*.

The original footbridge had diamond lattice guard rails on each side. To make a landing stage the guard rail on one side was removed. Since 1963 the downstream landing stage at Evesham has been extended twice, each phase being clearly identifiable by the different style back rail to the stage; the diamond lattice on the original stage is quite distinct. A photograph of the river at Tewkesbury from around 1920 shows the footbridge and its guard rails very clearly.

Overall costs of the Evesham job were £8,327. The lock was ceremonially reopened to

Evesham Lock reopening, 1963. Ribbon cut by E.P. Farr.

navigation by Mr E.P. Farr, chairman of A.E. Farr Ltd, on 7 June 1963. A small convoy of boats, including the 'official opening' 23ft river launch *Bluebird,* now in the Waterways Museum in Gloucester, and the former Evesham steamer (by then converted to diesel engine) *Gaiety* with a hundred Trust members and patrons on board, proceeded upstream to the new limit of navigation at Offenham, where a formal welcome was given by the Chairman of the Parish Council.

Apart from the mundane day-to-day tasks necessary to keep the Navigation functioning, this concluded the events of 1963.

The middle and late 1960s – more odds and ends
To say that the remaining years of the 1960s were uneventful would be doing a grave disservice to those involved in the continuous day-to-day work of keeping the Navigation running. Inevitably the pace of change slowed down – after all, what little was there still to do by way of reconstruction? However, they were busy if largely unspectacular years, at the end of which Barwell resigned as Chairman of the Trust Council. There was, of course, a substantial amount of debt to be repaid, both for the works of 'the last 600 yards' and the Evesham Lock restoration, amounting to over £6,000 – this had to be a priority.

The process of achieving a sound financial basis by means of registration of craft was in hand, although it would take a further eight years to achieve. Meanwhile every source of fund-raising had to be pursued: from persuading river users to take out Annual Lock

Passes (there was no legally enforceable system of user-paying available to the Trust), to recruiting new members, direct appeals for money for this or that improvement, sweepstakes, dances, raffles, collection boxes at lock-sides; everything was tried. It is fair to say that without these somewhat fragmented money raising efforts, which involved large numbers of people, the Trust would have had a very difficult time and progress would have been almost impossible.

Repairs were needed at Strensham Lock House, initially to keep it tenable, but the rear wing of the house was showing signs of bad settlement. The eventual solution, in 1969, involved demolishing the wing and rebuilding it as a single storey, at a cost of £2,000, funded by loans.

In 1963 an old vertical lift sluice gate and the adjacent river bank near Healings Mill at Tewkesbury suffered a foundation failure. Had the bank breached, the river level between Tewkesbury and Strensham would have been severely affected. No one accepted responsibility for this old sluice gate, so the Severn River Board stepped in and took prompt action. They removed the sluice altogether, as its operation had been largely superseded by the new and larger sluice gate at Stanchard Pit, installed in the 1930s; the whole main dam in the area was remade at a cost of some £12,000. As the Trust benefited from this work it agreed to contribute £1,500 towards the cost. The footbridge which spanned the old sluice was moved to Evesham, as explained earlier in this chapter.

The main dam at Pershore between the lock and weir was an earth dam backed by a stone wall and largely held together by tree roots; it was constantly eroded by boat use. Its condition caused concern during the weir repairs in 1962. In 1965 it was piled and the wall behind repaired. This not only strengthened the dam, it also provided, after dredging, a good upstream landing for lock users. The cost was £1,600, funded in part by a generous loan.

In 1963, Barwell learned from founder member and former Vice Chairman, Sir Reginald Kerr, who was then Chairman of British Waterways, that a number of small tugs were surplus to British Waterway's requirements, and would be sold by tender. In due course, *City* (more fully described in Appendix I) was bought by Barwell and delivered to Kempsey on the River Severn. The purchase money was partly recovered by others, including R. Burrowes, S. Goodby, R. Harrison, D.C.B. Mathews and R. Wimbush taking up 'shares' in *City*. Over time those shares have reverted to the Trust, which is now effectively the owner. *City* has performed, and continues to perform, valuable service in moving the Trust's work boats around and beyond the Lower Avon as required.

A positive move was the generous purchase, by Council Member R. Harrison, of the land adjacent to Wyre Lock, formerly owned by J. Whitehouse, and on which the Trust had to be very careful not to trespass during the lock restoration in 1954. The land was given to the Trust and has proved a most valuable asset, now providing greatly needed overnight moorings.

A new limit-of-navigation at the Bridge Inn Offenham, on the Upper Avon, was formally established during 1964, although the more adventurous could and did travel further upstream.

A census of every craft afloat on the river one Sunday in July 1965 produced a surprising total of 1,315 vessels.

The decision was made in 1964 to replace the Lock Cottage at Avon Lock Tewkwsbury, which was very dilapidated and beyond economic repair. This had to be funded by a twenty-five year mortgage with the then Tewkesbury Borough Council. The Trust wanted, and Tewkesbury Council required, the house to be built above flood level. The new bungalow-type house and office, built in 1965 on an elevated concrete platform, was completed before the autumn floods of that year surrounded it. It stands literally high-and-dry today, guarding the Navigation's 'front door' from the River Severn. An extension to the house was constructed in 1981 to accommodate a part-time peripatetic relief lock-keeper.

Cases of excessive speeding on the river were reported, and some instances of water-skiing. The Worcestershire County Council bye-laws being prepared would eventually control this nuisance.

At the end of 1965, the Trust Secretary R.W. Anstice retired because of ill health. He had efficiently steered the Trust's administration for the past six years, since the retirement of E.J. Price. I.M. Beard MBE was appointed in his place.

During the summer of 1966 there was a slight reduction in river traffic compared to the same period in 1965. Poor weather in July and August, together with a recent tax increase on the price of petrol – the main fuel used in boats at that time – was blamed. It resulted in an adverse toll income difference of £942 for the year – quite a serious blow.

Yet more appeals were made, particularly to boat owners on the river, and users of locks, only about half of whom were Trust members, to take up membership with covenanted subscription and Annual Lock Passes. The Trust felt, quite rightly, that these non-members were deriving benefit from the Trust's work without giving it financial support. Appeals were also made to Sailing Clubs: generally their members did not use the locks, but the main dams, most of which were maintained by the Trust, retained the water levels essential for their sailing. Riparian owners, some of whom abstracted water for spray irrigation, were also approached. It was impossible to quantify the results of these efforts, but it can be said with certainty that without them, the Trust's income would have been much less.

The Trust Council was becoming concerned at the apparent lack of orderly control over riparian development, which could adversely affect the beauty, tranquillity and landscape appearance of the river. In June 1967 the Trust organised an inspection cruise from Evesham to Tewkesbury for members and officers of the Severn River Authority, Worcestershire and Gloucestershire County Councils, Pershore Rural District Council and Tewkesbury Borough Council, which was well received by the guests. It was the forerunner of several subsequent inspections, which later proved to be of great importance, and which led to further satisfactory joint meetings with Planning Authorities at which all agreed that 'riverside development in open countryside should be restricted.'

Further dredging was required at Nafford and in the Pershore Lock channel; a new landing stage at Chadbury and repairs inside Wyre Mill to the main water retaining dam cost £2,500 in 1967. Also in that year it was noted that the annual income from tolls was £2,561 (£2,307 in 1966, £2491 in 1965), which barely covered those costs in spite of an

Avon Lock, Tewkesbury. The lock and lock house in 1999.

10% increase. Furthermore the costs excluded provision of new balance arms at Pershore and Nafford. On a more positive note, it was reported that 'our navigational works have stood up remarkably well to a season of high activity,' and that forty new members were elected, bringing the total membership of the Trust to over one thousand members for the first time.

During the autumn there was some anxiety concerning the new deflector wall at Fladbury, the base of which was beginning to be undercut by the flow from Fladbury Weir. This was remedied by tipping more stones of average weight $1\frac{1}{2}$ cwt along the weir side of the wall, in the corner by Cropthorne Mill, and along the weir side shore of the island. To tip these large stones precisely where they were wanted, a temporary narrow gauge railway track was laid across the lock approach channel and along the top of the deflector wall. The stones were loaded into tipper trucks and pushed along the track to the required position. This work has very effectively stabilised the structure.

In the 1968 New Year's Honours List, Foreman Munn was awarded the British Empire Medal to the general pleasure of all who knew him.

In July 1968 there was a very heavy rainstorm in the Avon Valley resulting in a flash flood. Fortunately no one was drowned, although a number of boats had to be abandoned by their occupants. A depth of 2ft 6in over the A44 main road near Pershore Bridge, and 4ft 9in in the B4080 road depth indicator boards by Eckington Bridge was noted. A large amount of debris: tree branches, fencing posts, oil drums, boxes, landing stages and small boats was swept down the river to be caught up in trees, hedges, and lock and sluice gates. Upstream of Nafford a whole field of newly made hay was swept away, much of it ending up in Nafford Lock. This alone took two men three very hard and long days to clear. Many volunteers responded to calls for help to clear obstructions from all along the Navigation, some spending several days on the job. Not only were there visible above-ground and water obstructions, there was also more silt and other debris trapped below water level. The Trust's regular quarterly Council meeting had to be postponed until the following month. Subsequent restitution works at several sites involved the use of long-handled scoop shovels which taxed the muscle power of many volunteers: the names Birchley, Bryant, Burrowes, Harrison, Humpage, Hackett, Johnstone, Rasey, Sallis, Street, Wilcox and Williams are recorded.

During this time work was currently proceeding on the construction of the M5 motorway bridge at Bredon, the clearance of which had been previously agreed.

C.R.P. Raymer, a founder member of the Trust, died in September 1968. An accountant by profession, he was Assistant Treasurer and closely involved in the Trust's administrative affairs from the start; he often took part in working parties on the river. For many years his office in Avon Street, Evesham was the Registered Office of the Trust.

At the end of the year Bathursts ceased to operate their fleet of thirty-five hire craft based at Tewkesbury. This was a mixed blessing: the loss of revenue was serious, but the poor condition of many of the craft had caused problems for the Trust.

Bathursts, established in the late nineteenth century, was, in its prime, Tewkesbury's principal boat building and operating business; it was also the only major boat builder on the Avon. Around the turn of the century, and up until the First World War, the steamers *River King* and *River Queen,* licensed for 192 and 168 passengers respectively, offered regular services to Gloucester, Worcester and beyond, and occasionally up the Avon. Later motor launches were built and operated, as were skiffs and punts, many of which were sent all over the country.

From 1926 to 1940 the business was owned by the Goodby family, as told elsewhere. The Robinson family bought the business in 1940; they came from Oulton Broad, Norfolk, where they had a flourishing boat building and hiring business. During the Second World War, many Admiralty contracts were completed for the building and repair of a wide range of vessels. Some of the Robinson hire fleet was moved from Oulton to Tewkesbury: wooden motor craft of various sizes and two sailing vessels. In the early days of this operation one vessel at Oulton and a similar one at Tewkesbury shared the same engine between them on alternate weeks – engines were probably unobtainable at this time. Current business parlance would doubtless describe this as flexible use of resources!

1969 brought nothing of great significance to the Trust. Barwell told the Trust Council in January that while he intended to retire as Chairman of the Council at the next Annual Meeting, he did not intend to retire from working for the Trust. To that end he was having built to his specification a new, self-propelled workboat, which he could take from site to site and from which he could work at whatever lock-side tasks were required. In due course *Avon Jubilant* appeared, which was used initially by Barwell and subsequently by volunteer maintenance gangs. She continues to give valuable service.

Fladbury Lock, 1967 – stabilising of the deflector wall. Small stone is unloaded sttraight from the workboat. The railway was later used for tipping larger stone on the weir side of the wall.

Concern continued over the Trust's sources of income. It was essential that membership subscriptions should not be allowed to lapse, and that wherever possible they should be enhanced and covenanted, and that new members should be recruited. This was the particular responsibility of Trust Secretary I.M. Beard. A scheme was devised whereby he derived a very modest commission on membership renewals and new memberships obtained. Its continuance was considered worthwhile for both parties. The Trust's annual dance, and a new sweepstake, were important, though small, sources of income.

During the year two stalwart supporters and Council members died. They were W.J. Beecham of Tewkesbury, of whom mention has been made earlier in this story, and F.W. Allen, whose name appears many times as a member of working parties in the 1950s – he was also among the guarantors of the Trust's frequent overdrafts and took a shrewd overview of the Trust's finances.

There were not many, if any, public bodies at this time empowered to make grants to organisations like the Trust. It was not a 'Club', its activities were not a recognised 'sport', or 'art', or 'cultural'. However, after long negotiations, the National Council of Physical Recreation offered a grant of £1,363 for eleven landing stages for lock access, estimated to cost a total of £2,726. This was a real breakthrough which would help provide a much wanted amenity; the balance would have to be met by a special appeal. The stages would be erected during 1970.

The post-restoration 1960s were clearly years of steady 'consolidation of gains' to use Barwell's words: piling of Pershore main dam; a new lock house at Tewkesbury; a rebuilt part of Strensham lock house, plus many minor improvements to various Navigation works. An increasing recognition by local authorities and others of the value of the Trust's work to the wider community was of great significance, and likely to influence public attitudes towards other restoration schemes elsewhere. All this consolidation was achieved in spite of hand-to-mouth finances.

This time also gave an indication of what the coming years would bring: concern over finances not helped by high inflation levels; planning control over riparian development; increasing numbers of craft using the locks, many of which were hire craft in inexperienced hands; continuing and constant maintenance of works, which from time to time would produce a need for a major refurbishment at a particular site.

Part IV Consolidation
10 The 1970s

To the great delight of all his friends, Barwell was awarded the OBE in the 1970 New Year Honours List.

The January 1970 Council meeting was the last taken by Barwell as Chairman. A wide range of subjects was discussed: proposals for an M1-M5 motorway link near Bredon Hill – long since abandoned – which could have passed near to or even over the river, objections to which were made through the Worcestershire Branch of the Council for the Protection of Rural England; proposals – again abandoned – for a new bridge at Eckington, the old bridge being by-passed by the river. Beecham Marine Ltd, of which Cottrell was a director, had offered to give land to the Trust at The Gouts, Tewkesbury, immediately north of Stanchard Pit, for the eventual construction of a new lock which would bypass the very low King John's Bridge. The offer was gratefully accepted. The land was conveyed to the Trust in 1972. Site investigation works, including trial bore holes, were later carried out by 62 CRE (Construction) Royal Engineers; their recommendation was that costly foundations would be necessary for large-scale works.

It was reported that the engine of the *City* had been overhauled and the bottom painted.

At the meeting H.T. Dumbleton was made an honorary life member of the Trust in recognition of his many hours filming and showing his films for fund-raising in the 1950s; a presentation was later made to him at the July meeting of the Council.

At the Annual General Meeting in March 1970, Barwell confirmed his previous decision to stand down as Chairman of Council. Many tributes were paid to him and a presentation was made to him and Mrs Barwell by Robert Aickman, a founder member of the Trust, and founder and Vice-President of IWA.

The April 1970 Council meeting elected a new chairman, H.S. Goodby, JP. Now retired, he had been active in public life, and was a Birmingham City Alderman; as a young man actively involved on the river, his family had had a controlling interest in Bathursts, the Tewkesbury boat builders and hire craft operators, until 1940. He was licensed as a skipper and engineer for passenger carrying craft on the Avon. He had known the Navigation in its heyday, its decline, and its recent restoration.

Goodby's declared aims were to foster good relations with the Upper Avon Navigation Trust, whose restoration progress was currently being made upstream towards Bidford-on-Avon, to strengthen the Trust Council and to spread the work load of the Trust over more and smaller committees.

Barwell was elected as 'the first Lifetime Freeman of the Lower Avon Navigation exempting him from all tolls, dues, charges and licence fees which may be levied now or in the future.' It was also agreed, but alas never implemented, that on retirement from the Council, he would be made the first President. As a mark of respect to him, that Office has never been filled. The office of Vice-President was also formally established, although left vacant for the time being.

At the July Council meeting Goodby appealed for more new people to come forward to help in different ways: professional and technical men and women with experiences in various fields to help with fund-raising, publicity and in other spheres. Fund-raising continued; a 200 Club was formed, which if successful would raise over £2,000 a year.

A gift of riverside land for overnight moorings at Craycombe Corner was made in 1972 by founder Council member K. Gill Smith, who had kept a rowing boat in a boat house on the site during the 1920s and 1930s; he always called the site Craycombe Turn.

At the same meeting forty-eight new members were elected, bringing the total membership to 1,026. Membership was constantly being eroded by death, members moving away from the area and other circumstances, so the drive to maintain overall numbers was both strong and successful.

A blow was the decision by Goodby in July that for health reasons he would retire as Chairman of Council at the end of his existing term of office in April 1972. He had had the unenviable task of succeeding Barwell, but he had very successfully led an individualistic council through quite an eventful two years, introducing a number of administrative innovations. He achieved an immense amount of vital and unspectacular behind-the-scenes work.

At the April 1972 Council meeting I was elected Chairman of Council, and E.S. Goodall became deputy chairman. H.S. Goodby continued to serve on the Council, and R. Sankey Smith took my place as Chairman of the Works Committee.

Having been closely associated with, and partly responsible for, most of the restoration works, I was lucky to have a fairly detailed knowledge of the Navigation, and of how the Trust was organised. I was also fortunate in living locally by the river, of working in Evesham, also by the river, of having served as member of Pershore Rural District Council, and in senior positions in a national trade association.

My aims were to build on the achievements of my predecessors, particularly strengthening the Trust's links with Local Authorities and other outside organisations. The restoration of the Navigation had been achieved; the great big outside world owed the Trust nothing; the Trust had to establish a new credibility as a self-funding Navigation Authority; its outlook had to change from being a do-it-yourself restoration society to that of running an amenity business. At the same time its navigation structures had to be maintained to the highest possible standards.

The Trust had an active, enthusiastic and experienced, albeit ageing, Council whose attitude would need to change gradually towards broader objectives.

The major event of 1972 happened in August with the granting of bye-laws by the Secretary of State for the Environment. A small point to note is that the relevant role of the former Ministry of Transport had been taken over by the new Department of the Environment, whose Minister of State was the Rt Hon. Peter Walker, Member of Parliament for nearby Worcester. Later in the year the Trust's bye-laws were formally signed and adopted. The detail of this vitally important event is told in Chapter 8.

When the new Registration Scheme was imminent in April 1971, I.M. Beard was appointed as acting Registration Officer to develop the administrative systems required, in addition to his duties as Trust Secretary. A permanent part-time Registration Officer, W.S. English OBE was appointed early in 1973. Mr. English had recently retired as Director of Luddington Horticultural Research Station.

1973 was the first full year of operation of the Registration Scheme. It produced an income of £9,861 from 1,587 registered boats. (In 1999 the income was £92,288 from 3,302 registrations.) The smooth running of the scheme in its first year, with so few initial problems, owed much to the firm and courteous approach of the new Registration Officer.

The first registration charges were based on the old voluntary toll charges and by 1974 had remained basically unchanged for four years in spite of massive inflation. The Trust had set itself six basic tasks:

1. To operate as an independent Navigation Authority.
2. To continue to maintain Navigation Works to an acceptable standard.
3. To carry out minor improvements and additions when required.
4. To make adequate provision for major lock repairs (e.g. replacement of lock gates) on a planned basis – now becoming necessary.
5. To establish an Emergency Reserve Fund. A river navigation is subject to natural hazards, like flood and storm damage, which can be very costly. It was felt that these should be covered by an emergency fund.
6. To make provision for new capital works which might (and almost certainly would) be required in the middle/long term (e.g. an additional Lockkeeper's house, new maintenance equipment, etc.)

If these tasks were to be achieved, it became clear that there would have to be a substantial increase in registration charges for the following year. In the summer of 1974 I commented: 'to have kept the charges at the same level for four years in a time of great inflation may have been a kindness to those who have to pay the charges, but was not a financially prudent (non) action from the Trust's point of view!'

Increasing costs in 1975 were a constant reminder of the need to increase income, which had to come mainly from boat users by means of registration fees. Users had been warned to expect substantial increases. Obviously these fees could not be set at a level which would drive boat users from the river, but they had to be at the highest level that the market would stand. Users had to pay more. In turn, the Trust had to give value for money to those registration fee-payers.

1975 saw the implications for the Trust of the new Health and Safety at Work Act of 1974. The Trust had to take this matter very seriously. Not only were the requirements of the Act both desirable and essential, they were mandatory; there were severe penalties for non-observance of the Act. A Safety Policy Statement was published, which was later revised in 1996. A programme of installation of 'aids that are intended to make our Navigation both safer and easier to use' was instigated 'as rapidly as financial and physical resources permit.' All this was going to cost yet more money. Council member R.G. Cranston was appointed Safety Officer; he also served in that capacity on the Upper Avon Navigation Trust.

The formal reopening of the Upper Avon Navigation in 1974 by HM The Queen Mother completed the last link of the 'Avon Ring': the Upper Avon, the Stratford-upon-Avon Canal, the Worcester-Birmingham Canal, the River Severn and the Lower Avon.

This 109-mile, 130-lock round journey, with great effort and long hours, could be accomplished in one week, although allowing two weeks made it a much more pleasant trip.

Many boat owners and hirers of boats made the journey. A steady annual increase in numbers of hire and private craft wanting short term registrations resulted. A number of hire craft operators established bases at different locations around the 'Ring', some on the Lower Avon. Such increased activity led to a welcome increase in registration income; the Trust could be said to rely on the continued existence of the 'Avon Ring' for a significant part of its income.

Much later, in 1977, I commented that without the 'Avon Ring' the number of short term registrations from visiting craft, the volume of traffic and resultant income would be considerably less. Events in 1978 proved me wrong. In March, following severe settlement, Alvechurch aqueduct on the Worcester-Birmingham Canal was closed for repairs for six months, which in turn closed the Canal itself and thereby the 'Avon Ring'. Approximately forty hire craft from the canal occupied temporary bases on the Lower Avon Navigation. Traffic, which formerly moved in one direction around the 'Ring, made a return journey, almost doubling the usage of the Trust's installations. Surprisingly, the absence of the 'Ring' made little difference to overall traffic volume

In 1979 Shortwood and Wast Hills tunnels on the Worcester-Birmingham Canal were closed for repairs for the whole season, thereby continuing the closure of the 'Avon Ring', with the same consequences for river usage as those of 1978. The summer months of 1979 saw an increase in lock usage of some 20% on the corresponding period the previous year.

Craft registrations in 1978 had shown a considerable increase, even allowing for the involuntary increase caused by the canal closure. The hitherto declining trend of private craft registrations was reversed, enabling 1978 charges to be held for 1979.

The Trust's team of experienced advisers was greatly strengthened in 1973 by the addition of W.G. Munn, and in 1975 by L.W. Haines.

W.G. Munn, BEM, usually known as, and referred to in this story as, Foreman Munn, retired from British Waterways at the end of 1973. He had spent his working life of fifty-three years with the River Severn Commissioners – later to become DIWE and then British Waterways – based at their Diglis workshops in Worcester, and since the late 1940s as Foreman. His father also served fifty-six years in the same job, also retiring as foreman. With his team, Foreman Munn had made and installed all the new lock gates on the river since the inception of the Trust twenty-two years previously, and had patched and nursed the old ones too. He had also been involved with other major works on the river and his advice was invaluable. The Trust appointed Foreman Munn as Consultant/Clerk of Works, on a very modest honorarium, so that his lifetime of practical experience and advice could continue to be available to the Trust, which was helped by him until a few months before his death. He died in June 1984.

On many occasions, when the Trust had sought advice or discussed its problems with the Severn River Board, later the Severn River Authority and then the Severn Trent Water

Authority, among those who listened patiently and offered help and advice was L.W. Haines, latterly Chief Engineer to the Severn River Authority and then Divisional Manager of the Severn River Division of the Severn Trent Water Authority. Mr. Haines retired from the Authority in March 1975 and happily accepted my invitation to join the Trust in a part-time executive capacity. Initially his title was Personal Assistant to the Chairman, as we reckoned that should give us both freedom to tackle anything and everything as required! Mr Haines was later referred to as Engineering Consultant.

His experience, capabilities and superb negotiating skills, together with his first hand knowledge of the Avon, were of inestimable value to the Trust in many different ways until his eventual retirement in 1996, when he was elected a Vice-President.

The 1970s saw vast expenditure on maintenance and repairs to the tune of £173,000, of which £64,000 was for one major repair. The detail of these works is described later in this chapter. The scale of works expenditure underlined the desirability, even necessity, of the appointment of Foreman Munn and Mr Haines.

In 1974 the Trust had a number of questions to ask – and answer – about itself:
Was it just amateurs 'having fun' running a river navigation? Or should it be a Navigation Authority, saying clearly to the new Local Authorities, and the new Water Authority, both of which would come into being during the year, exactly what it wanted the river to be and how it saw its future over the next twenty-five years? Was it now a business, the demands from the customers of which required a full time professional staff working under the direction of the Trust's elected officers?

What place had the Trust's volunteers (without whose help, both in the past and currently, the Trust could not manage) in a perhaps 'reorganised' Trust? Was a Charitable Trust, run by elected members, the best way of carrying the work of the last twenty-three years forward into the next quarter century? Ought the Trust to be financially viable from registration charges? Was this possible? Many of these questions are probably still pertinent today, twenty-seven years later!

During 1978 the Trust's committee structure was changed. The system which had served well for twenty-seven years was cumbersome. Instead of various responsibilities being delegated by the Council to several sub-committees, it was given instead to nominated individual members of Council, each of whom would discharge his responsibility as he thought fit. These nominated members of Council collectively became an Executive Committee, which could respond rapidly to events, and which reported to Council. It also made more effective use of members' time.

In January 1979, the Trust's Executive Committee looked again in detail at the questions posed back in 1974 about the future management of the Trust. It concluded, not unanimously, that while 'new blood' was needed, the Trust's existing way of working could and should continue.

1975 was the Trust's Silver Jubilee – its twenty-fifth year – which was celebrated in September with an informal reception. Around a hundred and seventy people, including nine of the original thirty subscribers to the Articles and Memorandum, spent a very enjoyable evening. There was a display of over forty photographs, showing the eight lock sites as they were in the early days and during the restoration process, and some superb aerial photographs taken of the locks earlier in the year – all of which caused great interest.

A Jubilee Souvenir Brochure was also produced which sold for £1, and H.T. Dumbleton's films of the restoration were edited and incorporated into up to date cine film of the river by D. Gittins.

The Trust had good reason to celebrate its achievements. The River Avon was the first river in England to be made navigable by means of pound locks (1635-1665). The Trust had continued the tradition:

> It was the first Navigation (or other similar project?) to be restored by volunteers (1950-1962).
> It was the first project of its kind to be managed by volunteers.
> It was the first to use armed forces (Royal Engineers 1952-1953) for a Civilian Aid Project.
> It was the first restoration project of its kind to be financed almost entirely without public funds.
> It was the first Navigation Authority to build a new (as opposed to replacement) lock-keeper's house in the United Kingdom in the last fifty years (1972).
> It was the first project of its kind to survive to its Silver Jubilee (1975)!

1976 saw the driest summer on record. It was fortunate that the Avon received – and continues to receive – a large volume of treated effluent from Coventry and from other large towns on its banks, which enabled very low flows to be maintained and the Navigation to remain open. In many places, Canal Navigations had to close through lack of water or were open only for very restricted hours. The Southern Stratford Canal closed to traffic in early July, which caused a decline of short term Lower Avon registrations. The prolonged dry weather saw great activity among craft based on or near the Avon, and led to the temporary establishment of additional numbers of hire craft on the Navigation.

After the dry summer of 1976, 1977 produced two summer floods, which clearly showed the potential hazards of a river navigation to the unwary. Large increases in numbers of hire craft on the river during the past three years, many crewed by people with little or no experience of rivers or canals, meant that at any given time during the boating season there could be hundreds of people afloat. Thanks to prompt action taken by the Trust's lock-keepers and others, no loss of life or of boats occurred, although some craft had to be abandoned. Talks were held with the Police Authority and Water Authority in an attempt to ease this unpredictable problem.

The numbers of craft did cause problems at times, with bottlenecks and congestion at certain points at peak times. Some of these problems could be eased, but the size of the river itself could not be changed. It was a tribute to the lockkeepers and those helping them that traffic kept moving smoothly, and to the general standards of maintenance that there were no major breakdowns of the Trust's installations.

For some years the Trust had been concerned about the very heavy work load of the permanent lock-keepers during the boating season. On busy days they could be working literally from dawn until after dusk. They were all recently retired people, unpaid, who had taken on the job out of interest; their only bonuses were very modest expenses and a

1975 Jubilee souvenir brochure.

Avon Lock, Tewkesbury, 1975. Picture taken to mark the Trust's twenty-fifth anniversary.

Strensham Lock, 1975. Picture taken to mark the Trust's twenty-fifth anniversary.

rent free house. To ease their load by trying to provide undisturbed off-duty hours, a controversial decision was made in 1978 to restrict the use of manned locks 'after hours'. Other benefits of the restriction allowed more accurate records to be kept of craft passing through the locks, greater safety, diminution of damage, and the prevention of registration evasion. While there were objections from the IWA and from some individuals, in general the scheme worked well. It was reviewed in detail at the end of the season and with some modifications continues to this day.

At the Annual General Meeting in March 1979, the retirement of Barwell from the Council was announced. Nine years previously he had retired as Chairman of Council and since then had worked indefatigably for the Trust, overseeing the Avon Lock job together with Haines, collecting vital information for talks with the Department of the Environment and Local Authorities about boat numbers, their movements and moorings, and doing a number of lock-side maintenance jobs. He continued to take a very close interest in every aspect of the Trust's work. Visitors to his house at Eckington were questioned in great depth, and on occasion exhorted to take suggested courses of action! Importantly, he started to edit his personal records of the Trust, the final version of which is now in the Worcestershire County Record Office.

In April 1979 D.J. Smith was elected Chairman of Council. Retired as General Commercial Officer with the Midlands Electricity Board, he had been Vice-Chairman for

Trust Council meeting, October 1975. Standing, from left to right, H.F. Paterson, assistant treasurer, R. Taylor, H.C.F. Barnham, R.J. Turner, treasurer, W.F. Tunna, R. Sankey Smith, D.C. Watson, A.W.B. Sayce, G. Morris, D.C.B. Mathews, E.S. Goodall, A.G. Belcher, J.C. Cluley, D.J. Warner, L.W. Haines, assistant to chairman, D.V.S. Cottrell. Seated, I.M. Beard, secretary, B.W. thompson, C.D. Barwell, founder, R.F. Aickman, J.Sanders, D.H. Burlingham, chairman.

two years and the Trust's official lecturer for several years; he had a good knowledge of the Trust and its work.

The 1970s – Many and various costly works

It was largely Goodby's drive that led to the building of the new lockkeeper's house at Evesham. By 1970 active consideration was being given to the future need to establish a control point at Evesham, for the time when the Upper Avon would be restored and generating traffic from upstream. A conventional brick built bungalow or house would need substantial and expensive foundations and would need to be raised above flood level, so alternatives were examined. A timber 'A' frame house which needed minimal foundations was the favoured design. The legs of the 'A' could be extended to give raised height; simple foundations and the fact that it was partly prefabricated meant a comparatively low cost. Outline planning permission was obtained in 1971 and thought was given to how it could be funded.

Continued progress of the Upper Avon restoration, which was formally reopened upstream to Bidford-on-Avon in June 1971, spurred the urgent need to raise money for the lock house, and by the summer there was sufficient money to enable an order for the prefabricated house to be placed at an approximate cost of £8,000. The contract, which was not without its peculiarities and difficulties, was supervised by J. Sanders and me.

By early 1972 the minimal foundations required for the new house were completed, and negotiations with the Trust's neighbours there, Robirch Ltd, successors to Collins Bros (Evesham) Ltd, for sewerage connections, were also completed.

The new house was completed in the early summer. The new lockkeeper, J.H. Brittain, a retired journalist and former war-time naval officer, did much to turn a building site rapidly into an attractive home, office, lock-side and garden. As the Trust was already negotiating with the Department of the Environment on proposed government policy changes, advantage was taken of the occasion to ask the Minister of State for the Environment, the Rt Hon. Peter Walker MP, to formally open the house, and while he was on site to make sure that he, as well as his civil servants, were well aware of the Trust's concerns. The lock house was the first new – as opposed to replacement – lock house to be built in the United Kingdom for over fifty years.

A running five-year schedule of remedial work was presented to the Council in July 1970, and works agreed for the next twelve months, but as with so many well-intentioned plans, its requirements were largely overtaken by urgent needs caused by floods, increased lock usage and other factors beyond the Trust's control.

1971 began with a long, whole-day works inspection by the Trust's Works Committee which I remember well for two reasons: the first was that it was one of those rare perfect cold winter days with a hard frost and brilliant sunshine – everywhere glistened in the strong light and muddy areas were iron hard; the second was that we discovered that a whole weir had disappeared! The inspection started at 8.30 a.m. when we all piled into Cottrell's Landrover and travelled from site to site beginning at Evesham; much walking was involved, but we were able to get to most places, and probably see more from ashore than from afloat. When we came to Nafford, having carefully examined both lock and weir, I suggested that while we were in the immediate area we ought to take a look at Berwick Brook and its weir. Berwick Brook is a curious watercourse – the only one now of its kind on the Lower Avon, although similar ones are found on the Thames and several East Anglian rivers. It flows *out* of the main river on the Birlingham side about two hundred yards below Comberton Quay; it flows over a small weir and rejoins the main river below Nafford Weir. It is shallow, slow flowing and in summer partly choked with reeds. The works committee walked the length of the brook from below Nafford Weir to its upper confluence near Comberton Quay – we should have seen the weir near the upper confluence but we hadn't. I had last seen the weir, a modest brick and stone structure, about ten years previously; it was small, not on the main river, and of little consequence – out of sight, out of mind. Some of the inspection party took some convincing that there should be a weir at all, especially as it could not be seen. After poking about in the brookside undergrowth, eventually we discovered masonry walls on opposite sides, but nothing between. The weir had disappeared, clearly some years previously, and no one had noticed or even missed it! The inspection continued downstream to Strensham and beyond until darkness, and concluded with a working supper during which a works programme was drafted. It was a long day, fourteen hours, but well worthwhile.

Evesham lock house 1972. Slating the roof.

The weir's absence was reported to the Severn River Authority, which built a new structure of stone filled gabions, the Trust contributing half the cost. This structure was later replaced in 1996 by the Environmental Agency. The 1971 rebuilding required a five day closure of the Navigation in May. While water levels were temporarily lowered, some non-urgent repairs to Nafford Weir and the upstream adit walls of Nafford Lock were carried out.

During the 1971 inspection, the very poor condition of Chadbury sluice was noted, and on more detailed examination, it was found to be on the point of collapse. Its existence was necessary for the very occasional drying off of Chadbury Weir for inspection and repair. Immediate consultations with the Severn River Authority and Evesham Town Council confirmed the Trust's view, and both agreed to contribute one third of the cost of repairs and of subsequent maintenance. A change of ownership of Chadbury Mill, sluice, weir and lock island had just occurred. Following negotiations with the new owner, the lock island, weir, sluice, and a small piece of land by the sluice were given to the Trust, along with a sum of money equivalent to one third of the cost of the repairs. The new owner, who was very helpful, was relieved of a substantial potential liability, and the Trust gained full control of vital structures. Repairs to the sluice were planned for the following year and were carried out in June 1972. A full detailed description of the work is given in Appendix H.

Lock keepers house, Evesham, built over the sluice channel adjacent to lock.

Paddle gear breakdowns during 1971 prompted the overhaul of all paddle gear before the next season. The Strensham Swing Bridge was rebuilt. Also, and significantly during the year, suggestions had been made to consider the 'mechanization' of lock operation at the manned locks.

In 1971 and 1972 the Trust was having difficulty in obtaining the services of Foreman Munn and his team; their employer, British Waterways, had a very extensive works programme on the Severn and were very reluctant to release them, even on a contract basis. There was therefore an immediate need to identify a general contractor who would be able to tackle some of the more unusual aspects of the Trust's needs. P. Williams & Sons of Defford, who had shown both ingenuity and application at Chadbury sluice, became the clear choice.

Worn paddles were replaced at seven locks in 1972, and timber was ordered for new top gates at Fladbury Lock, which were installed the following year. Substantial repairs were made to weirs at Pershore and Evesham, and new treadwalks under the balance arms were laid at Evesham and Fladbury Locks. Further improvements were made to the maintenance wharf at Wyre, revetment work at Wyre Weir and Wyre Weir island was done. A formidable list of additional work was identified for 1974.

During the 1974 winter there were major works at Strensham Lock. The whole lock chamber plus the basin below the lock was dewatered. Work included a new floor, and an apron at the lower end with new cills. The top gates had new mitre posts and new rails and paddles fitted. The underwater part of the swing bridge plinth was rebuilt. The water supply pipe to the house and lock-side was incorporated in the new floor, and underwater hydraulic pipes were installed for subsequent mechanization.. The cost of these works was £8,000; the contractor P. Williams & Sons.

At Nafford major works were also carried out by P. Williams & Sons in 1974, where the lock was piled off, dewatered, and both ends of the lock rebuilt and refloored, enabling future stanking off to be done safely and efficiently. The gates were re-planked, extension paddle gear, new safety hand rails over the gates and new steel balance arms were fitted. Concrete walkways were laid round the lock-side and two new landing stages constructed.

The balance arms at Nafford were the first on the Navigation to be converted to steel, which offered considerable cost savings when compared with traditional English oak. The steel was second-hand channel section, set on edge, flange to flange, and joined at intervals to make a rigid box section. As other balance arms needed replacement, the same general specification was used, until the introduction of purpose-made steel box beams at Wyre in 1997 and Evesham in 1999. Only history will tell which is the better option!

At Pershore in 1975, a new pair of top lock gates was fitted, together with steel balance arms all around. At Evesham the top gates were re-planked, new safety rails were fitted on the gates, and new concrete walkways were laid round the lock-sides at both Pershore and Evesham. At Tewkesbury the lower landing stage was entirely reconstructed as a three level stage, necessary to accommodate fluctuating Severn levels. New landing stages were also constructed on the land leased to the Trust by Tewkesbury Town Council, which not only improved the facility, but also the appearance of the area. As a condition of the lease, overnight mooring charges collected appear in the Trust's subsequent annual accounts as 'Donation by Tewkesbury Town Council'.

Following the major works of 1974, Strensham Lock was mechanised in 1975. The installation was hydraulic, with a single pump and control system supplying an operating ram at each gate and each paddle making a total of eight rams. The gates had been modified during the preceding winter job, with an additional paddle hole in each to accept an hydraulically operated paddle; the original paddle holes and manual paddle gear were retained and are now back in use. Severn Trent Water Authority contributed £4,500 towards the cost.

The poplar trees at Avon Lock, a feature of the site but unsuitable for it, were felled in the winter, fortunately before severe gales in January 1976.

Major repair work at Avon Lock, Tewkesbury was the largest single project ever undertaken by the Trust. Work had been postponed from the winter of 1975-76 because preliminary investigations indicated that more extensive work than originally envisaged was needed; more time would be needed to plan both the work and its funding. The work was now urgent: the Healings side lower wing wall was on the point of collapse, and the lower lock gate on the same side was fast becoming inoperable, which would mean closing the lock to all traffic.

Before deciding to proceed, development of a new lock on land at the Gouts was considered. Site investigation by 62 CRE (Construction) Royal Engineers in 1973 indicated possible problems on this site, reference to which is made earlier in this chapter. The time required to design, obtain planning consent and build a new structure was likely to be much longer than that to make full repairs to the existing lock. Even then, full repairs would take over six months. The risk of additional delays was too great to take. It was hoped that the work could be done during the late autumn and winter months.

Nafford Lock, 1971. Repairs to upstream adit walls, taking advantage of lowered water levels.

Because of the size and complexity of the job, Barwell and Haines, rather than a committee, were asked to manage all aspects of it, reporting to the chairman and Council. Barwell made it quite clear that his emergence from a quite active 'retirement' was not to be construed as a return to active Trust involvement.

In May 1976 the Council accepted a tender of £37,000 from Thomas Vale and Sons Ltd (the main contractors for the Wyre Lock restoration in 1954 and the deepening of Fladbury Lock in 1957). This sum covered temporary cofferdams, pumping, the provision of a steel-piled right-hand downstream end, and a mass concrete replacement of the out-of-true wall by the downstream end right-hand gate and other minor items. The cost of mechanization was not included, nor was work that might need to be done when the lock was dewatered.

Before accepting the tender, the Council was satisfied it could meet demands for stage payments as they arose. That this could be done was due, to a large extent, to the prompt and generous response of Trust members and well-wishers to an Appeal for interest free loans and donations. 1977 and 1978 income would fund a loan redemption account.

The lock was closed to traffic on 13 September 1976 and work started immediately. For safety reasons the whole site, including the public footpath across the top gates, was closed to the public. An Open Day for Trust members to see the dewatered lock was held on 30 October. Several floods during the winter covered the site, stopping work for a total of thirty-two days. The lock reopened to traffic on 16 April 1977, only sixteen days behind schedule.

An electro-hydraulic system to mechanise the lock operation was installed during the summer of 1977. Learning from the experience of mechanisation at Strensham, the electro-hydraulic system eliminated the need for long runs of hydraulic pipes; it comprised four separate power packs mounted on brick plinths and controlled electrically from a central point.

Nafford Weir, 1971. Revetment of scoured end of weir crest using stone filled gabions (large wire mesh baskets). In the foreground is the crest of the dried off weir.

The overall cost of the whole project, including mechanisation, a new lock floor, a new downstream left side quoin, a new upstream ground paddle, substantial rebuilding of the lower lock gates, repairs to the top gates, new upper end stank slots and walls, plus four mooring piles, amounted to £64,109.

The very substantial expenditure on locks and other installations during the previous four years meant that in 1977 and 1978 the Trust's income could be largely devoted to funding Avon Lock, as only minor works were needed elsewhere.

During 1976 safety hand rails on lock gates were installed at Chadbury, Fladbury and Wyre, concrete walkways were laid on lock-sides at Fladbury and Wyre, and fire extinguishers were provided at the three manned locks and on workboats.

In 1978 a major concern was the condition of the lias stone walls of the lock chamber at Evesham Lock, which were almost on the point of disintegration in places. They were treated with Gunite, a sprayed reinforced concrete. At the same time both pairs of lock gates were re-planked and experimental steel paddles fitted. These latter were found to be unsatisfactory in use and were later replaced with timber. Also in 1978 Chadbury Lock was dewatered, the gates re-planked and the cills repaired. At Fladbury new collars were fitted

Strensham Lock, 1974. Top gates with new mitre posts, rails and additonal paddle holes for subsequent hydraulic operation. Foreman Munn is on the left.

to the gates and the old timber quoins upstream replaced in steel; these quoins proved satisfactory in use, as well as simple, quick and comparatively inexpensive to install. One balance arm at Fladbury was replaced with steel. At Wyre Lock the downstream return walls had been badly damaged by boats, and were rebuilt and fitted with substantial fendering; new landing stages were constructed upstream and downstream. The downstream approach to Wyre Lock was – and is – notoriously difficult because of the discharge from the weir. At Pershore parts of the main dam were strengthened with stone mattresses, and parts of the lower approach channel revetted with gabions.

Safety measures taken included installation of ladders at Evesham and Chadbury Locks. The Severn Trent Water Authority installed floating barriers at their Nafford and Tewkesbury sluice gates.

The upstream approach to Evesham Lock along the 450ft crest of Evesham Weir had always been difficult, and was a potential hazard at times of increased flow after rainfall. A barrier along one third of its length was considered an essential safety feature, and was installed in August 1979.

Pershore Lock, the deepest on the river, with the underwater deepened parallel section, and above water semi-diamond shape, took a very long time to fill through the two top gate paddles. With boats in the lock, the paddles could only be raised gradually, otherwise the boats would be swamped.

During the 1978-79 winter, a ground paddle discharging into the parallel side of the lock bottom was installed – quite a major job in itself – and the volume of the lock was reduced by raising the parallel underwater sides to full height. By opening the ground paddle, the water level in the lock could be raised without turbulence until the gate paddles were submerged and could be opened safely. This resulted in a much quicker operation, eliminating part of the peak-time bottleneck for users. Other minor repairs were carried out.

During 1979 at Strensham there was serious concern about movement in the island side lock chamber wall. To stabilise this wall it was decided to tie the lock wall to the bank on the far side of the lock island. This bank anyway required trench sheeting to withstand heavy use as a landing stage and anchor piles could readily be incorporated; tie bars were laid across the width of the island. A finger landing stage was constructed upstream.

While on site the Trust's contractors also built a new bank-side lower landing stage at Strensham, and then another at Fladbury, comprising steel trench sheeting, backfilled and concrete capped. This type of stage better withstood the constant heavy usage of steel hulled narrow boats. Extensions were made to the downstream landing stages at Pershore and Evesham.

For all these major works, apart from Avon Lock, the main contractor was P. Williams & Sons. Over the decade they had acquired a considerable – and in most cases a literally in-depth – knowledge of the Trust's sites. Also, of inestimable value, they could, did, and still do, turn out at very short notice for emergency repairs.

The 1970s was very active for works on the Lower Avon. A wide range of jobs were tackled: from the extensive Avon Lock works at Tewkesbury, through lock gate renewal on other sites, to the many and varied day-to-day repairs, the control of which needed constant vigilance. The overall expenditure during the period was over £173,000.

During this time, on occasional weekends and holidays, I travelled nearly all of the then available inland waterways on my narrow boat, and was able to see and use for myself the whole range of different lock systems and associated works. In 1974 I wrote in *Avon News*: 'With the possible exception of the River Thames, I have yet to find a Navigation consistently maintained to the comparatively high standards of the Lower Avon, and one where all the locks are easily accessible and light to work. ...I consider the Lower Avon is at least as good as any other Navigation.'

By the end of the 1970s the Trust could be well satisfied, but not complacent, with its installations.

The 1970s – Working with others

September 1970 saw the third inspection cruise of the river from Evesham to Tewkesbury for local authority members and officers. The vessel used was *Gaiety*, and the event was regarded as a great success by the Trust and its guests. I remember that I acted as commentator, talking about the various locks, weirs and other works as we passed by or through them. I also remember that we stopped to rescue a calf that had fallen into the river near Chadbury and could not get back onto the bank; this was quite a hazardous procedure involving several of our guests and a long rope; it had the merits of entertaining our other guests and saving the calf! To pass through the navigation arch of Eckington Bridge, the skipper decided to go stern first: the bow was anchored to the bank (which was realigned some years later), and the anchor cable slowly released to allow *Gaiety* to slip gently through the very tight-fitting arch. This journey to Tewkesbury was the first time for forty-one years that *Gaiety* had travelled the full length of the Navigation.

This inspection trip for local authorities resulted in an increased grant in 1971 from Worcestershire County Council. The problems of identifying places for permanent and overnight moorings were pressing. Goodby, Cottrell and the Secretary attended a joint meeting with six local authorities, from which a planning policy would be devised.

Following the Trust's earlier discussions with Planning Authorities in 1972, Worcestershire County Council approached the Trust in connection with its Avon Valley Study and Report, on the draft of which the Trust was asked to comment. Principal Planning Officers were given a full day private inspection of the whole River Avon by boat. This form of all day contact encouraged and allowed full and confidential discussions which led to much greater mutual understanding by all parties.

The County Council later published *Worcestershire Countryside Studies No.3 The Avon Valley*, a report concerning every aspect of the Avon Valley, intended for planning policy guidance. Contacts with the County Planning Officers were maintained, although with impending changes in local government administration the new Planning Authority for most of the Lower Avon would be the new Wychavon District Council, and in Gloucestershire, the new Tewkesbury Borough Council. An increased single grant in 1973 from Worcestershire County Council of £4,000 was very welcome. From this time forward, the Trust was routinely consulted on riparian planning applications.

As the Trust was developing and changing, it was important that close co-operation was established and maintained with all sorts of 'outside bodies'. A very considerable amount of Trust Council senior members' and officers' time was now being spent in this way; the Trust was providing an increasingly valuable service to the community in running what was becoming a 'linear water park', and it was important that members and officers of local authorities, the general public and the Trust's personnel and members recognised this.

In 1974 Trust members, river users and other interested bodies had to be reminded that the Trust had no control – it has none now – over the number of registered boats on the river. Any craft in respect of which the Trust has received a satisfactorily completed registration application form, for which the appropriate registration fee has been paid and which complies with the terms of the bye-laws, must be registered by the Trust. When the bye-laws were being drafted, the Trust wanted to take powers to refuse registration in appropriate circumstances, but such powers were not granted.

The only way in which numbers of boats based on the river could, and can, be controlled was by the (non) availability of permanent moorings, and this, in turn, was controlled by the relevant Planning Authorities. Early in 1974 the Trust made the following recommendations to a joint meeting with County and District Planning Officers:

1.   That there should be no further commercial mooring development either bank-side or off bank on the Lower Avon, or sailing/boating club development;

2.   That three areas of the river (Chadbury – Fladbury; Cropthorne – Wyre; Tiddesley Wood – Eckington Bridge) should be very carefully conserved. (These three areas were the only significant lengths of river to remain completely unspoilt at this time.);

3.   That where existing moorings were near locks, there should be no increase in numbers of craft;

4.   That every encouragement should be given to 'visiting' craft (i.e. those not based on the Lower Avon) to travel the river for short periods.

These recommendations clearly showed the Trust's commitment to conservation, even at the cost of restricting potential growth in registration income.

Since the mid-1960s there had been talk and discussion in government circles of reorganising water supply and sewerage services. Land drainage and possibly inland navigations would also be affected. There were Green Papers, White Papers and other proposals. These would eventually be incorporated in a Bill to become the Water Act 1974, which saw the establishment of Regional Water Authorities. Much time was spent responding to consultative papers. No mention was made, at this stage, of inland navigations. Because of this uncertainty, the Trust was concerned to make its views very clearly known by submitting a very detailed Memorandum to the Department of the Environment in 1972, with copies to anyone of influence – Local Authorities, Members of Parliament and our own members. Following the formation of the Severn Trent Water Authority, which had assumed the land drainage responsibilities of the Severn River Authority, both Upper and Lower Avon Navigation Trusts each gave a full day river inspection on sequential days to the Chairman, Vice-Chairman and senior Land Drainage Engineers of the new Authority's influential Land Drainage Committee. This proved to be of great benefit to all parties.

In March 1976 a consultative document (Green Paper) *Review of the Water Industry in England and Wales* was published. Suggestions were made that independent navigations should be taken over by a new National Navigation Authority. Strong representations continued to be made to the Department of the Environment; in May the Parliamentary Under Secretary, Kenneth Marks MP, together with senior civil servants from the Department, was given a whole day inspection of the river by boat. About this time, in view of the implications of being 'taken over', the Trust had a professional valuation made of all its properties, which as well as locks, weirs and sluices, also comprised three lockkeepers' houses, Wyre Mill and some parcels of riverside land. Unfortunately all the papers relevant to the valuation were destroyed in the 1998 flood.

In 1979, a new Parliamentary Under Secretary at the Department of the Environment, Marcus Fox MP, announced that '…the Government did not propose to merge the waterways into the Regional Water Authorities.' Mr Fox, with senior civil servants, had spent a whole day on the river with the Trust the previous year. The Trust's efforts, which involved several Trust people for a number of whole days as well as many hours at other times over seven years, had succeeded.

A proposal in October 1974 by Aickman for the creation of a 'Shakespeare Water Route', in conjunction with a Federation of the National Trust (then lessees of the Southern Stratford Canal), the Upper Avon Navigation Trust, and the Lower Avon Navigation Trust, to attract substantial government grants for maintenance and improvement of the three Navigations for large-scale tourism, was explored in some depth. The details of the idea were not acceptable to the Trust and the matter was not pressed. It remains one of the more intriguing 'might-have-beens' of inland waterway history.

```
┌──────────────────────────────────────────────────────┐
│          THE LOWER AVON NAVIGATION TRUST               │
│          ───────────────────────────────               │
│                                                        │
│             INSPEDTION OF LOWER AVON                   │
│                    by water                            │
│            EVESHAM to TEWKESBURY.                      │
│                                                        │
│             3rd September, 1970.                      │
│             ────────────────────                       │
│                                                        │
│                   PROGRAMME                            │
│                   ─────────                            │
│                                                        │
│  09.00 prompt   -   Depart Evesham                     │
│  09.40 approx   -   depart Chadbury Lock               │
│  10.30 approx   -   depart Fladbury Lock               │
│  11.15 approx   -   depart Wyre Lock                   │
│  11.20 approx   -   arrive Wyre Mill Club (toilets)    │
│  12.00 approx   -   depart Wyre Mill Club              │
│  12.45 approx   -   depart Pershore Lock               │
│  14.15 approx   -   depart Nafford Lock                │
│  15.00 approx   -   arrive Strensham Lock (toilets)    │
│  15.30 approx   -   depart Strensham Lock              │
│  17.00 approx   -   arrive W.J.Beecham (Marine) Ltd.,  │
│                             Tewkesbury.                │
│                                                        │
│  NOTES:                                                │
│  ──────                                                │
│        1.  As the vessel has no toilet facilities      │
│            on board, stops will be made at Wyre Mill   │
│            Club and Strensham Lock, where facilities   │
│            are available.                              │
│                                                        │
│        2.  A packed lunch will be issued with the      │
│            compliments of the Trust. A bar will be     │
│            available on board; the Trust regrets non-  │
│            complimentary. Tea will be served, again    │
│            with the Trust's compliments, at Strensham  │
│            Lock.                                       │
└──────────────────────────────────────────────────────┘
```

Inspection cruise for local authorities, 1970 – programme.

The 1970s – Summing up the decade

So ended the industrious and exhilarating 1970s. It was a time of high and fluctuating inflation, averaging 11% with peaks of 27% and 22% which did not help financial forecasting. Nevertheless, achievements of the decade included: the establishment of a Registration Scheme enabling self-funding of day-to-day costs; a new lockkeeper's house, good contacts with the Department of the Environment and Local Authorities; well-maintained locks, two of which were mechanised; and a very large growth in river traffic. Credibility as a progressive Navigation Authority was established. There was still, and always would be, a need for constant monitoring of the Trust's structures and a continuous need to repair and replace worn parts of the whole; funds from outside sources would always be needed for new projects.

It was 'plus ça change, plus c'est la même chose' but there was just more and more of it!

11 The 1980s

The 1980s and 1990s in very general terms were a repeat of the 1970s: steady vigilance and constant maintenance, the cost of which was just covered by income. Opportunities to obtain grants from outside bodies for specific projects were greater, and these were sought with a fair degree of success.

The 'Old Guard' of stalwarts, D.C.B. Mathews, and J. Cluley, continued on the Trust's Executive Committee; other long time staunch supporters, R.F. Aickman, E.S. Goodall, K. Gill Smith, J. Sanders, and R. Sankey Smith sadly died, most serving until their last illnesses; others remained on the Trust Council, but in a non-executive capacity. 'New blood' was found, and together with some of the 'old guard', continued to run the Trust.

The work load of the Secretary gradually changed and increased. There were new requirements of Charities and Health and Safety legislation, clear records of decisions and actions had to be kept, grant opportunities had to be identified and pursued. The addition of part-time paid maintenance staff during the period meant a more rapid and less costly response to routine maintenance work. Costs of larger scale works projects continued to increase.

A catalogue of repairs, paddle replacements, lock gate re-planking or even lock gate renewal, and occasional dredging makes dull reading. For those directly involved, or those with a managerial function, it was steady, unspectacular hard work. There is little glamour in repairing some minor breakdown when the site is left just as it was before the event, yet without that attention the whole installation could not work; the same observation applies equally to administrative work. Sadly many river users rarely know or even care about what is involved in operating a river navigation. It is rather like a drinking water supply: when the tap is turned, water appears; it is taken for granted.

So rather than relate a long and somewhat repetitive list of the Trust's activities during these last twenty years, the following three chapters seek to highlight the more significant happenings. These took place against a background of continuous dull routine of both works and management, which was only very occasionally broken by an unusual event.

The 1980s – people

R.F. Aickman, the London-based author and literary agent from the very beginning of this story, who was a founder Trust Council member and founder Chairman and later Vice-President of the Inland Waterways Association, died in February 1981. He was a very loyal supporter of the Trust and rarely missed a Council meeting in spite of having to travel from London on most occasions. His comments and advice on waterways matters were always pertinent, and his confidential observations on waterways personalities enlightening. He left a small legacy to the Trust which was used towards the cost of building a dumb barge (perhaps an inappropriate choice of vessel for such an eloquent person!) which was named after him *Robert Aickman,* and which is one of the Trust's vital items of equipment.

Another Trust stalwart who died during this decade, in November 1987, was R. Sankey Smith. An electrical engineer by profession, he was elected to the Trust Council in 1954 and brought a very keen and enquiring mind to the Trust's Works Committee, as well as offering very practical hands-on support of early volunteer working parties.

G.V. Clarke died in September 1981. An Evesham man, he was a founder member of the Upper Avon Navigation Trust, a Council member of UANT since 1977 and, following his retirement from work in 1979, Chairman of UANT. He was elected to LANT Council in 1980. His business career had made him an outstanding negotiator and administrator; he was a man of great integrity, loyalty and sincerity. The tragically short time he was on the LANT Council did not allow his full potential to be used, which was a great loss. Had he lived the whole saga of 'amalgamation' and whatever may have led from it, might have been different.

In 1983 the Trust elected a new Chairman of Council, D.H. Stokes, a retired Chartered Accountant with great dinghy sailing interests, a long-time active supporter of the Trust and for the past year Trust Treasurer. His immediate predecessor, D.J. Smith, had presided successfully over four very active and sometimes difficult years.

At the same time there was a change of Trust Secretary. I.M. Beard MBE had worked under four successive chairmen: Barwell, Goodby, Burlingham and Smith, and over almost eighteen years had seen and been involved with many changes. His personal views very occasionally conflicted with Trust policy, and at times he could be 'difficult', but he was a very able administrator and very loyal to the Trust. His knowledge of Trust matters was encyclopaedic. He died in 1996.

The 1980s: – Problems – dispute with Association of Pleasure Craft Operators
During the early 1970s, throughout the midland waterways system there was rapid growth in the numbers of hire craft being built and operated. A private individual could purchase by mortgage a steel-built narrow canal boat, which was then leased to a hire craft operator. A proportion of the hire charges obtained was used to repay the mortgage. This arrangement could be fiscally advantageous to some tax payers. The purchaser had the 'free' use of his boat for an agreed period, while the lessee operated and maintained the boat. This arrangement provided a significant amount of interest-free capital for rapid expansion of hire craft fleets.

By 1973, the first full year of mandatory registration and the first year for which figures are available, the numbers of hire craft registered and based on the Lower Avon, in proportion to the numbers of private craft registered, was growing steadily.

Private craft tend to be used relatively infrequently and mostly at weekends and on bank holidays. Even then the maximum number of private craft likely to be away from their regular mooring at peak times does not exceed one third of their overall total number.

Hire craft, on the other hand, need to be earning hire fees for their operators over as long a period as possible. When a vessel is hired, the hirer obviously wants to get maximum use for the charge he has paid, and the vessel will be in use and travelling for a large part of the hire time. In the mid-1970s a hire season was reckoned to be twenty-nine weeks – from about Easter to mid-September. The period is now much shorter, but that is irrelevant to this particular part of the story.

In the late 1970s and early 1980s there were an increasing number of hire craft – mostly steel hulled narrow boats – being used almost continuously over the 'season'.

In 1973, eighty-one hire craft and 1,500 private craft were registered; in 1980, the peak year, the numbers were 281 and 1,334 respectively. Subsequently the numbers changed very significantly and by 1990 they were 48 and 1,092 respectively.

These large numbers caused problems for the Trust, in particular because of the very heavy usage of the locks, largely by relatively inexperienced users, and in some instances by users who had received no, or only very poor, instruction. The wear, tear, and frequent damage was costly, not only in terms of money, but in the disproportionate amount of time taken to handle a large volume of relatively small, but nevertheless essential repairs.

These increasing costs were becoming a financial worry to the Trust by 1980. Between 1973 and 1980 registration charges for hire craft had increased by only modest amounts each year, keeping just ahead of inflation, but not recognising the increased usage. It was these craft, not the private craft, that were causing most of the damage; it was only right that they should pay proportionately more than they were doing.

In 1981, the Trust announced what can only be described in retrospect as swingeing registration fee increases for hire craft, in many cases of over 100% on the charges for the previous year. Naturally the hire boat operators objected, and through their trade association, the Association of Pleasure Craft Operators (APCO), tried to get the Trust to reduce the charges. Many operators either withheld the registration fees in protest or only paid a proportion of them. The Trust contended that the increases were justified. Unfortunately, stalemate was reached and the dispute passed into the hands of solicitors. All depended on what increase in registration charges was considered 'reasonable' in the circumstances. Counsel's opinion was sought by both parties. The Trust would not meet representatives of their disgruntled clients, represented by APCO, to discuss the matter. A summons was issued and a date set for a Court hearing to decide what might be a 'reasonable' increase.

Before the date set for the proceedings, common sense prevailed: representatives of the Trust and APCO met on several occasions. The matter was eventually resolved, with reductions in the proposed 1981 charges and agreement on percentage increases for 1982 and 1983; the Trust also agreed to consult with APCO 'about subsequent changes in tolls.' The agreed increases were just sufficient to cover the increased costs and anticipated future costs; they would not recompense the Trust for recent past cost increases, which it had barely covered from income. The Trust had ignored the fact that it was a business similar to any other, and that ordinary commercial practices required that a supplier (in this case a monopoly supplier, the Trust – albeit a registered charity) must maintain good relations at all times with his customer – in this case the hire craft operators represented by APCO.

Good relations with APCO continue, although the numbers of hire craft based on the Lower Avon are now very small, under thirty. The numbers of visiting hire craft, most of which take out short-term registrations, remain steady.

The 1980s – More problems – sabotage

The large volume of boat movements in the late 1970s and the 1980s disturbed the peace and tranquillity of the river, and threatened to destroy the qualities which made it so attractive. A more serious side to this was what was described in minutes and reports as 'vandalism' (of which there was certainly some at various sites), but which I firmly believe were deliberate attempts at sabotage. Events happened in March and May 1980. In the middle of March at Nafford, one of the upstream gate straps (the 'hinge' which holds the gate back in to the quoin) had been deliberately loosened. When a boat tried to lock through, the gate, having no top support, collapsed into the lock damaging the cill. The gate was lifted back temporarily, but high water levels prevented a prompt full repair to the cill, which involved stanking off and dewatering the lock. Fortunately this work was completed before the Easter holiday. The event was fairly described as '...a stupid, wanton and dangerous act.' Remedial work cost £2,700.

The May occurence, which happened just before the bank holiday weekend, was caused by the paddle gear racks on both top gates being removed from site and the $1\frac{1}{4}$in diameter solid steel connecting rods between racks and paddles being sawn right through. While a temporary repair (about 5% efficient) was made, it was a whole day, with many scores of boats waiting to enter the lock, before full repairs could be completed.

The similarity of both events was more than a coincidence; it was, I believe, deliberate sabotage. No one was caught for these crimes and they were not repeated.

No one, to my knowledge, was ever identified or caught for these crimes, and the incidents were not repeated. They do, however, show that all was not sweetness and light on the river at all times, and that problems were not confined to careless or inexperienced use of locks and wear-and-tear breakdowns.

The 1980s – bits and pieces STWA's Flood Alleviation Proposals – 1984

In 1984, the Severn Trent Water Authority (STWA), then the body responsible for land drainage, was proposing a far reaching review of the Avon catchment area leading to proposals for a comprehensive flood alleviation scheme. It started consultation with a large number of interested parties, including the Trust.

About this time the STWA had just been 'privatised' and its former, somewhat cumbersome membership, both elected and appointed, which collectively had some comprehensive knowledge of local conditions, had been considerably reduced. Policy direction of operational matters had passed completely into the hands of officers, very few of whom had any local knowledge or background.

The driving force behind flood alleviation proposals was the farming industry. At that time production of agricultural crops was considered of great national importance. Where there was an acceptable cost/benefit to agriculture, such schemes were considered as long term projects.

The STWA's land drainage powers were considerable, and, in the extreme, could extensively change river management patterns and the appearance of the whole valley. The Trust's powers, in effect, were only the right 'to navigate'. Here was possible cause for conflict, or at best, compromise. The Trust, together with others, was very apprehensive.

One of the attractions of large parts of the Lower Avon is the ability to see over and beyond the relatively low lying river banks. In the early 1980s a flood embankment about one and a half miles long was constructed by the STWA just north of Birlingham. About six feet above the existing bank, and almost on the bank edge, it had the effect of obscuring the view from the river across the adjoining land. Had the embankment been constructed about fifty feet further back from the bank, its effect on the view would have been very considerably less. More poorly sited embankments could have a deleterious effect on the valley landscape.

Back in the mid-1970s the Severn River Authority had initiated the development of a 'mathematical model' of the Avon Valley. This was a computer programme designed to measure the effects of differing rainfall levels in different parts of the catchment area on the rates of flow and water levels at any point on the river and its principal tributaries. Conversely, the effect of altering river channels, removing or altering weirs, sluices and locks could also be measured. The effects of increased development of housing, industrial sites, road building and other factors could all be added to the data. The model was a very comprehensive aid to the production of cause-and-effect information needed for development planning and for flood alleviation. The SWTA had inherited the model and continued to develop it.

The STWA's findings in 1984 indicated that there was scope for improving the frequency of flooding (loosely defined as overtopping river banks) of some agricultural land, some routes across the valley and some properties.Interestingly, and significantly, the mathematical model also showed:

> There would be no benefit to flows in removing any existing structures (weirs, sluices, locks).
>
> There would be no advantage to flood alleviation in altering existing retention levels.
>
> There would be only limited advantages in increasing the flow capacity of structures.
>
> Enlargement of channels to carry increased flows would need to be very great.
>
> A preferred solution would appear to be a combination of some excavation (channel deepening/widening) and construction of embankments.

After the consultative meeting, at which I represented the Trust, I felt much reassured. In the event, no part of the proposed scheme was implemented. Economic changes since make its revival unlikely. The story of this proposed scheme is told to show the Trust's need for constant vigilance and maintaining good relations with other organisations.

The 1980s – River Safety Scheme - an ongoing concern
With increasing numbers of craft of all kinds and sizes on the river at any given time during the season, by the late 1970s the Trust was becoming concerned about the safety of their crews in time of floods. At the height of the season and during holidays there could be many hundreds of people afloat, scattered along the length of the river, some of them in remote and relatively inaccessible places. Many of these people would be unfamiliar with the area and inexperienced in the ways of the river.

At this time there was some uncertainty as to what constituted a flood; the condition meant different criteria to different people. To riparian land owners and the police it meant water levels overtopping the banks and spreading over adjacent land, thereby putting some people, livestock and some properties at risk; also closing some roads. To the boater it meant very much lower water levels but strongly increased rates of flow which made boat handling difficult and potentially dangerous for the inexperienced.

Most private boat owners recognised high rates of flow conditions, knew where to seek advice if they wanted it, and were experienced in boat handling. The converse was the case with most users of hire craft.

The Trust held discussions with the police, who, while being grateful of being alerted to the differing problems, did not consider it their task to advise and warn river users.

The Trust had no legal authority to 'close' the Navigation, nor to prevent the master of a private vessel using his craft under hazardous conditions; through its lock-keepers, it could only advise; most boat masters would heed such advice. Hire craft operators were in a slightly different position; they could, as part of their contract with their hirers, insist that the hirer conformed to advice given by authorised persons or by advisory notices.

Summer floods in June and August 1977, which produced the highest river levels since 1968 '…clearly showed the potential hazards of a river navigation to the unwary. Thanks to prompt action taken by our lockkeepers and others, no loss of life or of boats occurred, although some craft temporarily had to be abandoned.' This situation clearly prompted all interested parties to address the problem with some urgency.

Following joint discussions with all concerned parties and with the Association of Pleasure Craft Operators (APCO) taking the lead role, a warning scheme was devised which had the support, as far as they were able to give it, of both Upper and Lower Navigation Trusts. Basically the scheme consisted of two kinds of warning signs: at accessible sites such as manned locks, boatyards, and some moorings, a manually changeable fixed sign saying that navigation was dangerous; at less accessible sites, a vertical red (top) and green (bottom) board; when water levels covered the green area, conditions would be deemed hazardous. Operation of the manual signs would be triggered by the Severn Trent Water Authority (then responsible for flood control and land drainage) advising an APCO designated 'controller' or his deputy on 24-hour call that river levels at Warwick were one foot above normal summer levels. According to prevailing conditions, the 'controller' would alert a number of assistant controllers, each responsible for a sector of the river between Stratford-upon-Avon and Tewkesbury, and they in turn would advise people in their respective sectors to operate the warning signs. The police would also be alerted. Not all sections of the river would necessarily be affected at any one time. The signs could only be advisory, although hirers were required to obey them, and stay moored while conditions were hazardous. The role of the Trust was limited to its resident lock-keepers (three at the time of the Scheme's introduction, now two) operating manual signs at three – now two – locks, helping boaters as required, and reporting local conditions to the APCO 'controller'.

The scheme worked reasonably well for many years – it was revised in March 1992 – and is currently being revised again to take account of changed circumstances. Its efficiency relies almost entirely on the prompt operation and cancellation of the manual signs, and on the correct setting of the vertical red/green boards at each location.

The 1980s – larger works. Operation Wyre Dredge

The Avon, like any other slow flowing river, carries a large volume of silt in suspension during times of flood, and then deposits the silt in slow flowing places when levels fall. Normally the main river channel is self-scouring and this process is helped by the continual passing of boats, which keep much of the silt suspended and therefore on the move.

Backwaters tend to have little or no flow and are therefore susceptible to silting. The Trust's maintenance wharf at Wyre, requiring access by deep draft craft, in particular the Trust's loaded work boats, is sited at the end of Wyre Mill backwater. By the summer of 1984 it was apparent that the whole length of the backwater, just over two hundred yards would have to be dredged.

Normally this would be a comparatively straightforward job using a dragline excavator from the bank. At Wyre, however, both banks were lined with overhead electricity lines and with landing stages to accommodate Wyre Mill Club members' vessels, making access from the bank virtually impossible.

Consultations were held with a number of suction dredging operators, and other specialist contractors, all of whom either declined the job – it was only a very short distance to be dredged – or quoted very high prices.

Mark Williams, of the Trust's ever resourceful contractor P. Williams and Sons, was approached. He suggested an experiment, financed by the Trust, with a Case hydraulic excavator mounted on the Trust's workboat *Lantern.* In early November the experiment was tried, but the combination of the excavator and *Lantern* proved too unstable.

However, it was thought that if suitable craft could be secured alongside *Lantern*, the rig would be sufficiently stable. A search on the river eventually led to the Upper Avon Navigation Trust, which had two suitable vessels, the mud hopper *Cammell* and a steel narrow boat mud hopper. Agreement to hire these two craft was made, and with volunteer crews including J. Sanders and D.C.B. Mathews, they were moved from their Upper Avon sites to Wyre. Following a period of trial and error, the two Upper Avon vessels were satisfactorily attached to *Lantern,* providing a stable working platform for the Case excavator which could place dredged material into *Cammell* and the Trust's mud hopper *Robert Aickman.*

With a stable workable rig P. Williams & Sons were able to offer a satisfactory day work rate and work started on 12 November. By the month end the job was completed in fourteen and half working days of atrocious weather which caused two days to be lost by flooding. Almost 5,000 cubic yards of silt was removed. It was transported by boats towed or pushed by *City,* operated by J. Sanders and D.C.B. Mathews, to the wharf, and unloaded by another excavator into dumper trucks which tipped the material in an adjacent field. Wyre Mill Club contributed towards the costs.

Before the component parts of the dredging rig were separated and returned to their respective bases, encouraged by the success of the Wyre operation, it was decided to remove shoals upstream and downstream of Wyre Lock and upstream of Pershore Lock, which involved a further eight days work. On completion, cleaning the work boats, plant and wharf site took another four days. Altogether it was a very successful operation.

Wyre Weir 1987

Easter weekend 1987 saw some frantic activity at Wyre. During the previous week the river had flooded – not excessively, but enough to produce higher than normal levels and very strong flows. On Good Friday evening, 17 April, Trust Council Member D.C.B. Mathews, who kept his boat at Wyre Mill, noticed that a tree had lodged on the crest of the upper of the two weirs, and that a large part of the glacis, or sloping part, was being washed away. He reported this by telephone to L.W. Haines, who agreed to make an inspection the following morning.

Early the following morning, Mathews and Haines were joined by Simon Williams, representing the Trust's Contractor P.W. Williams & Sons, and together they made an inspection. It was clear that within a short time a complete breach of the weir would occur unless immediate action was taken; an unsuccessful attempt was made to remove the tree.

It was obvious to Haines that the depth of water flowing over the weir, about 12in, must be reduced quickly in order to slow the rate at which the weir was being scoured away. The only way to do this was to raise the six small sluice gates, which had not been moved for over thirty years. Simon Williams agreed to muster a gang, and to manufacture appropriate gear to attempt to raise the gates near Wyre Mill early the following day – Easter Sunday.

Haines considered that to make a proper repair it would be necessary to drive a row of piles part way along the toe or bottom edge of the weir, tie them back to three piled anchors, then back fill the scoured hole with selected hardcore and cap the whole with nine inches of reinforced concrete. This meant finding an immediate source of piles of the required length, and the appropriate water borne equipment from which to pitch and drive piles and to handle the materials…and this was during a long bank holiday weekend!

By 9.00 a.m. on Sunday the sluice gates were raised and the river level was reducing; by evening only two or three inches of water was flowing over the weir.

The Upper Avon Navigation Trust turned out to have suitable equipment for the job, a Mustang excavator, which they could operate from their workboat *Cammel*. They agreed to release both immediately from work at Stratford-upon-Avon, and they also had a stock of piles which could be used and replaced at a later date.

During Sunday a further site meeting with Peter Williams agreed the plans for the permanent repair works. David Hutchings, general manager of UANT, also saw the site and agreed that UANT plant and two operators could be safely employed.

On Easter Monday, UANT plant was on the move and expected to arrive at Evesham, a twenty mile journey from Stratford-upon-Avon, by evening. The reduced water level was being maintained, lessening the risk of a breach occurring and without severely affecting the moving of the vital workboats coming downstream to the site.

By Tuesday the detail of the work had been settled, the piles had arrived at the Trust's Maintenance Wharf at Wyre, and been loaded onto the Trust's workboat *Robert Aickman*, ready to be moved to site about five hundred yards away. By evening UANT's *Cammell*, with the Mustang excavator on board, had also arrived. A pile hammer and air compressor were to be delivered the next day.

Pile driving began on Thursday 23 April, and was completed the next day in spite of difficulties necessitating a new deeper line requiring longer piles. Help was given by the

Severn Trent Water Authority in the immediate supply of longer piles, and the works were inspected by the Chairman of the Authority's Land Drainage Committee, who promised continued support.

With a good weather forecast, a welcome and necessary weekend break was taken. The scour hole was filled with hardcore on Monday. All the materials, piles, hardcore and concrete had to be loaded into workboats at the Trust's wharf, then taken through Wyre Lock to site, unloaded and placed.

By the end of the second week the job was complete – including repairs to other parts of the weir, and to the other lower weir. Large stones were also placed along the lengths of both weirs as toe protection.

This was a remarkable event, showing how quickly a major potential catastrophe was prevented with the help and co-operation of many people. The consequence of a weir breach at Wyre, which could have happened within a day or so, could have been very serious: the Navigation closed for several months; possible bank slip in places – especially by Wyre Piddle village; the four miles of river upstream reduced to a small muddy trickle, affecting anglers, irrigation abstractors and many others.

P. Williams and Sons dropped everything at no notice to do the job; the Trust's tugmaster D.C.B. Mathews and his crew, the Trust's UANT neighbours, and the Severn Trent Water Authority all rallied round to contribute to this achievement. The smooth working and rapid successful conclusion of the job owed much to the professional skill and guidance of L.W. Haines. The Trust was indeed fortunate to have so much help and goodwill. The whole job cost £17,868.

Avon Lock Repairs

After the extensive repair work and mechanisation of Avon Lock, Tewkesbury in 1976-77, it became clear ten years later in 1987 that the lower gates, replaced in 1952 and adapted for hydraulic operation in 1976, would require renewal. Avon Lock was the deepest lock on the Navigation, and consequently its lower gates were the longest.

The lock was originally constructed in the seventeenth century and had to be deep enough to accommodate the levels of the tidal river Severn, which at that time was open without obstruction to the Bristol Channel and the sea. Navigation weirs and locks on the Severn were not built until the mid-nineteenth century, almost two hundred years later. The siting of Upper Lode Lock on the Severn, approximately three quarters of a mile downstream, effectively raised the Severn level outside Avon Lock by about three feet and reduced the tidal influence. Avon Lock was therefore now much deeper than was necessary.

If the lock floor level could be raised, the new lower gates could be shorter, would be easier to operate and would cost less. Another good reason for raising the floor level was that it would help to strengthen the deep lock walls, especially if the new floor was suitably anchored to the walls.

A new reinforced concrete floor was constructed 3ft above the original floor level, with the upstream end shaped to direct a smooth water inflow from the ground paddle. The lock walls, part brick, part sandstone block, the condition of which was poor, were treated with gunite, a sprayed reinforced concrete, and the top edges of the lock chamber were timber-faced.

New steel lower gates, now shorter than the old ones, were made locally and installed without too much difficulty. These new gates, as with other steel gates on the Navigation, had tubular head (mitre end) and heel (quoin end) posts. With the new floor level new cills were fitted.

The lock could only be filled by the operation of the unique horizontal ground paddle. While this had been adapted for hydraulic operation in 1976, its underwater parts were as vulnerable in 1987 as they had always been, requiring either a diver or stanking off for any underwater repairs. A single manually operated gate paddle was therefore fitted in the house-side top gate, by way of insurance should the ground paddle fail. Both top gates were re-planked.

On this occasion the weather was kind, and the job proceeded without the usual disruption from flooding.

Early winter 1999 saw Avon Lock dewatered again. The problem on this occasion was the condition of the wooden top lock gates. They were made and installed in 1961, had been repaired and re-planked on several occasions, and were now beyond economic repair. They were replaced with steel gates made by British Waterways and to their design, having timber mitre and heel posts. Both gates have manually operated paddles for emergency use. Avon Lock top gates also carry a pedestrian footbridge, the design of which was changed to make it more wheelchair friendly.

While the lock was empty, advantage was taken to install two vertical ladders recessed into the lock walls.

Consideration was also given to replacing the unique horizontal top ground paddle with a more accessible vertically operated paddle. The cost of replacement proved to be prohibitive.

12 The 1990s

The 1990s – People

Barwell died in November 1990, marking the end of an era for the Trust. He had retired as Chairman of Council in 1970, and from the Council in 1979. Questions are often asked about him; what sort of a person was he?

He was a man of vision, drive and enthusiasm, with apparently boundless energy. He was a practical common sense engineer and a shrewd businessman, both essential qualities for any restoration project. He was a clear and decisive thinker, having little time for theories which could not be put to practical use. He would listen to and accept advice from others, and when he knew he could safely delegate work and decision making he would do so; but he was the leader, and properly required regular reports and discussions on delegated projects. When he gave instructions they were clear and with as much detail as necessary; he expected those instructions to be carried out to the letter.

He was insistent that whatever work was done for the Trust, from general administrative work or promotional activities, to site works, whether just painting, fixing a simple bracket or a large scale restoration project, the highest standards were essential. Many times he would say: 'If we can't afford to do the job properly, then we wait until we can afford it.' Inevitably there had to be make-do-and-mend emergency repairs, but behind every plan was the counsel and practice of perfection. I cannot think of any non-emergency work done by the Trust that had to be revisited because of poor work, such was his high standard.

He had a very strong personality, and little sense of humour; you either got on with him or you got out. After some crisis I remember a colleague saying: 'In this job you either become resigned or you resign.' If you did disagree with him, and argued your case clearly, he would listen, and on those rare occasions when your case was better than his, he would accept it.

Basically he was a shy person, who suddenly found himself having to take a very exposed leading role. He reacted to this by becoming apparently rather autocratic. It was always 'I did…' or 'Your chairman has…' which did not always endear him at the time to the many Trust workers who also 'did' or 'had'; he appeared to take all the glory, while the troops just slogged. In fairness it should be said that if he had not pushed himself forward – and always on behalf of the Trust – much valuable publicity and general support would not have been forthcoming. His diaries show a generous appreciation of named individuals.

Barwell's contribution to the Trust, and through the work of the Trust to the inland waterways of the country, is incalculable. He was the right man in the right place at the right time. Three simple memorial plaques to him were erected in 1995 at Avon Lock, Nafford Lock and Waterside, Evesham.

There were other Trust stalwarts who died during the 1990s, all of whom played significant roles in its work and development.

Not a Council member, but never the less a very influential contributor to the Trust's history was Charles Beale, the Trust's solicitor. It was he who drafted the Trust's

Charles Douglas Barwell, OBE.

Memorandum and Articles of Association. The pattern of these Memorandum and Articles was followed by many similar organisations. Beale also took an active part in drafting the Trust's bye-laws, and, of course, acting for the Trust in its routine legal requirements.

S.J.G. Clover, who was also for a time Chairman of the Upper Avon Navigation Trust died in 1991; also R.G. Cranston, who was Council member responsible for Health and Safety on both UANT and LANT.

Two pillars of the Trust died in 1994: E.S. Goodall and J. Sanders.

Goodall was very active on the committees dealing with the restoration works at Wyre, Pershore, Fladbury and the 'last 600 yards', and was very closely involved in the 1952 'Save the Avon' appeal in Evesham. For many years right up to his death he was Deputy Chairman of Council, an unofficial office, but one which many Chairmen have been glad to consult; in that capacity he was always available for confidential discussions, and his calm considered advice was invaluable.

J. Sanders, boatbuilder and boatyard proprietor of Pensham near Pershore, was consulted by Barwell well before the establishment of the Trust. His knowledge of the river was invaluable, especially in the early days of the Trust when many of its active workers were still learning about the whole task ahead. His practical skills meant that his advice was practical too. He was an early member of the Finance and General Purposes Committee, which ran the day-to-day business of the Trust, and on the retirement of its second chairman, Trust Treasurer, P.H. Protheroe, he was elected committee chairman.

Just before his death, the Trust elected him as its first Vice-President in recognition of his great contribution to its work.

R.C. Ward died in April 1997. He had been Reachmaster at Nafford Lock since 1978, and was elected to Council in 1989 and became Deputy Chairman in 1994. His clear vision, firm attitude towards problems together with strong negotiating skills made a very positive contribution, but sadly he died before the Trust was able to make full use of his very considerable talents.

Betty Barwell, widow of Douglas Barwell, died in 1997. Wherever Barwell was, and whatever he was doing, Betty Barwell was always quietly in the background. The innumerable cups of tea she made for the Trust working parties must, in terms of volume, have been almost sufficient to fill a lock. When Barwell used his diving apparatus, it was Betty Barwell who controlled the air supply. It was she who ceremonially cut the ribbon to reopen the Lower Avon Navigation in June 1962. Barwell records in his diaries of the restoration: 'There are very many references in my Record Books of the activities in which she participated. I wish these Records to be read on a basis of OUR endeavours, culminating in a satisfactory and successful conclusion.' This says it all.

On a more happy note and to the great delight of his colleagues, in the Queen's Birthday Honours List of 1998, D.C.B. Mathews received the award of MBE in recognition of his outstanding contribution to navigation on the Avon.

T.W. Gray succeeded D.H. Stokes as Chairman of Council following the Annual General Meeting held in October 1989. A retired international industrial sales manager, he had owned a boat on the Lower Avon for many years and had become involved in helping Reachmasters at Chadbury Lock. He was co-opted on to the Trust Council the previous July.

Gray's major achievement was the formation of the Avon Weirs Trust, the story of which is told in Chapter 13. He also initiated the Way Forward Group, which started to look at the Trust's future.

He was succeeded in 1994 by Dr D.N.F. Hall, a retired international fisheries scientist. With long-held boating interests, he retired to live by the Upper Avon and had become a Council member of UANT. He led the UANT team in amalgamation discussions, described in Chapter 13, and in 1993 chaired the joint working group which produced the report *LANT/UANT Amalgamation – The Balance of Interests* in 1993.

Dr Hall largely succeeded in modernising many of the Trust's procedures in several areas; he was influential in bringing about the major improvements at King George's Field, Pershore. It was sad that he lost the confidence of a majority of Trust Council members and he resigned in 1999. He was succeeded by T.W. Gray, his predecessor.

The 1990s – various items

Walkways, treadwalks, mooring posts and safety rails are accepted today as normal; their provision is one of the very small marks of progress. Fifty years ago, they mostly did not exist. Treadwalks, or scorting rings as they are sometimes called, are the arced occasionally ribbed paths underneath the ends of lock gate balance arms. In 1950 there were none; there may have been a few large stones on edge, but otherwise only the ground surface of grass or soil. In dry weather this was just acceptable; in wet weather users pushed balance arms, their feet slipping in the mud beneath. Complaints of repaired lock gates being stiff

Strensham Lock garden, 1954, largely the work of Mrs Barwell, kneeling on right

or hard to operate were almost solely due to the fact that the user had no firm purchase on the ground with his or her feet. Initially, the Trust regarded treadwalks as a non-essential amenity. Increasing use of locks hastened their provision when circumstances allowed. A walkway in this context is defined as the surfaced area, normally of concrete, along the edges of the lock-side. Back in 1950 there were none. There were only the coping stones at the edge of each lock chamber. The land beyond did not belong to the Navigation anyway, and the amount of use of the locks, at that time more or less nil, did not require anything else. As locks were restored, one of the first 'aids-to-lock-use' to be installed were mooring posts on each lock-side. These were usually old lock gate timbers. They were later gradually replaced with scrap steel tube. Over time, as described elsewhere, the Trust acquired lock-side land, and with increasing use, lock-sides became potentially hazardous places with no firm or dry surface, especially in the areas immediately adjacent to mooring posts. Narrow concrete walkways were added, initially being no more than approximately two feet wide. Over the years they have been widened, and now all lock-sides have firm dry walkways all round.

The pattern of safety rails on lock gates has gradually changed over the years. In the pre-1950 years, on most lock gates, but not on all, there was a single horizontal handrail, which enabled anyone crossing the lock on the balance arms to steady themselves; they were not all sturdy enough to support a person's weight. As locks were restored and brought into use these plain single horizontal rails were fitted to all gates. Health and Safety legislation prompted provision of a more substantial tubular rail with two horizontals, and all lock gates were so provided by 1980. It was later felt necessary to fit this type of safety rail on both sides of each balance arm, thereby providing a narrow, double-fenced crossing over each lock gate. Exceptions to these patterns are on the top gates at Avon Lock, Tewkesbury, which carry a lock-side level cantilevered pedestrian public footpath across the lock mouth, and, since 1999, the top gates at Evesham Lock where a similar type crossing saves the lock-keeper from having to climb over the gates.

The provision of ladders in lock chambers was prompted by Health and Safety requirements.

A considerable variety of paddle operating gear is used on Lower Avon locks. Old photographs from around1900 show a distinctive direct-gear-to-paddle-rack fitted to most locks; this pattern has been retained for historic reasons at Chadbury Lock. Elsewhere there is a mixture of largely Trent and Mersey Canal and Birmingham Canal Navigation paddle gear. Once new gear of whatever pattern is installed it has a long working life.

The 1990s – Boat Safety Scheme
In the early 1990s the British Waterways Board (BWB) introduced a Boat Safety Scheme for all licensed craft on rivers and canals controlled by them. Initially the scheme applied to new hire craft, then to all hire craft and finally to all craft on their waterways. The scheme set very high standards for the installations and maintenance of Liquid Petroleum Gas systems and appliances, inboard engines, electrical systems, ventilation and many other safety aspects. The Thames Conservators – now the Environmental Agency – had been operating a much simpler Safety Scheme for many decades.

To obtain a BWB Licence, all relevant vessels had to undergo a rigorous inspection by a BWB appointed Examiner, who, if satisfied that the various sections complied with the tough BWB standards, would issue a Certificate of Compliance – now called a Boat Safety Scheme Certificate – which was valid for four years. At the end of that time, a further examination was required for renewal of the Certificate. Without a certificate, BWB would not issue a licence.

The effect of these onerous regulations was to improve very rapidly the varying (and sometimes unsafe) standards of installation and maintenance, and to make all BWB licensed vessels very much safer for their users.

The Trust noted all this, but being an independent navigation, BWB requirements did not apply on the Lower Avon, nor on the Upper Avon. However, it was felt in 1992 that in principle the Safety Standards were sensible, and that in due course they should be implemented on the Lower Avon, probably in conjunction with the Upper Avon Navigation Trust. Boat owners were regularly advised of developments; a 'flexible' implementation of the scheme was introduced in 1997, and full compliance with the regulations applied from 1998.

Temporary Moorings
Provision of overnight moorings for both private and hire craft away from base, and of landing stages for lock access, is an historical problem with which the Trust has had to contend. Over the years the Lower Avon has gained the now undeserved reputation that there are very few overnight moorings between Tewkesbury and Evesham.

In 1950 the Trust owned no land apart from the areas covered by each lock chamber, and that under the 'swing of the balance arms'; there was also the site of the cottage at Avon Lock, Tewkesbury. Lock-side land up to the coping stones on top of the lock walls was in other ownership. River banks between locks were, and are, privately owned, and most of the fishing rights from them have either been leased or sold to Angling Clubs. Moored boats and anglers

Avon Lock, Tewkesbury, 1952. At the time this was probably the second busiest lock on the river. Note the mooring post and lack of concrete walkways, only coping stones on the lockside and a muddy track.

do not always cohabit harmoniously. It is not unknown for Angling Clubs to buy riverside meadows at prices well exceeding their agricultural value, and then to resell the land at its true value, while retaining all fishing rights. There is no continuous bank-side public footpath or towpath along the Lower Avon – only a few isolated lengths. The proper procedures for boaters, more honoured in the breach than the observance, was, and is, to seek permission to moor from the owner, whose response might well be governed by the terms of lease or sale to an Angling Club. Land owners tolerated the use of lock adjacent river banks for access to locks, but only for that purpose, and not for longer stays.

By the end of 1950 the Trust had bought the derelict mill cottage at Strensham, to be restored as Strensham lock house, with some adjoining riverside land, but at that time there was no pressure for overnight moorings. The comparatively small number of craft moored where they could.

As the Navigation was gradually restored various sites became accessible. With Pershore Watergate demolished and Pershore Lock deepened, Pershore Recreation Ground, and the gardens of some Pershore hostelries, became easily accessible, as was the garden of the Anchor Inn at Wyre.

Until the river restoration was completed, provision of overnight moorings was not a priority; all monies raised were spent on restoration projects and lock maintenance. If gifts of land came the Trust's way well and good, but even acquisition in this way could be double-edged, as was clear at Evesham and Pershore with land adjoining the locks and weirs, when immediate and costly emergency repairs were required to the weirs – the stories of which are told elsewhere. Over the years the Trust did acquire small parcels of riparian land. Many of these sites, when acquired, were overgrown and had to be cleared and developed by volunteer labour, where and when feasible, to provide moorings.

While gradually building up this portfolio of land, the Trust also negotiated with Parish Councils and others for the use of some of the former parish wharfs. In more recent years considerable sums of money have been spent on providing good mooring facilities, both on Trust-owned and publicly-owned land. In the latter case improvements have usually been funded jointly by the Trust and Local Authorities.

There are now seventeen mooring sites on the Lower Avon, providing an approximate total mooring length of 4,250ft for travelling boats. This figure excludes visitor moorings provided by boatyards, marinas, and public houses. While this provision is just adequate for present use, the Trust is continually trying, with some success, to obtain the use of additional sites.

Collection of registration fees

With a large part of the Trust's income dependant on registration fees, it was important that the Trust received its dues promptly.

Annual registration charges cover a full calendar year. Many boat owners did not pay until either they had launched their boats, having had them ashore during the winter, or until they started to use them regularly; some did not pay at all either through forgetfulness, or in the case of a very few, through deliberate default. In the latter instances, they were in breach of the bye-laws, which require all craft afloat to be registered.

In 1999 a prompt payment scheme was devised which allowed a discount. This was an instant success and altered the whole positive cash flow side of the Trust's income. At the same time concessionary and reciprocal terms were agreed with British Waterways. For many years there have been reciprocal discounted registration rates with the Upper Avon Navigation Trust. These were very positive commercial achievements.

Slow payers have always been chased. Marina and boatyard proprietors have always been most co-operative with the Trust's Registration Officer; regular checks along the whole length of the river are made to ensure all craft carry a current licence. Defaulters are checked, traced, and pursued, and where necessary legal proceedings instituted. The first Court fine for non-payment of registration fees was for £600, plus £300 costs, and was imposed in 1997.

The Way Forward

During the 1980s the Trust's administration was busy with other everyday matters, and it was not until the early 1990s, when T.W. Gray became Chairman, that he felt it necessary both to look more closely at the Trust's internal workings and at the wider aspects of what the Trust should be seeking to do in the long term. He commented to Trust members in a Bulletin '…over the years the administration of the Trust has become somewhat fragmented, so we are at present looking at ways to control this work, with priority being given to the day-to-day activities which influence the Trust's income…'. Various aspects of the Trust's internal administration were being changed from manual to computer systems. A small group of Trust members, experienced in the Trust's workings, formed a Way Forward Group (WFG).

The ongoing work of the Trust clearly took priority over consideration of long term aims, particularly problems with weirs and the formation and direction of the newly formed Avon Weirs Trust, so while some progress had been made with administrative matters, long term requirements were not addressed.

Shortly after Dr Hall had succeeded T.W. Gray as Chairman of Council, the WFG produced Terms of Reference and a Mission Statement which were approved by the Council.

> LANT's Mission: To provide a safe and efficient navigation on the River Avon from its confluence with the River Severn upstream to and including Evesham Lock and weir, at a cost acceptable to the licence payers, bearing in mind the need to co-operate with all users of the river, and to seek with them to protect and enhance the aquatic and riparian environments.

With the Mission Statement there was a 'Schedule of Areas for Consideration' which included among other matters: Executive Responsibility of Directors – with recommendations, Communications and Public Relations, Organisation, Control of Costs. All these matters would need the careful consideration of the Trust's Executive Committee and Council.

From discussion of the 'Schedule of Areas for Consideration', Codes of Practice were devised and approved for various Trust functions, which in January 1997 were incorporated into a Manual of LANT Procedures. This manual clearly laid down what should be done by whom and how.

A clear Mission Statement, such as the Trust now had, together with the Manual of LANT Procedures provided a firm base for the future day-to-day operation and management of the Trust.

It did not attempt to address the longer term problems: What was the future of the Lower Avon Navigation Trust? Why are so many people involved in operating $28\frac{1}{2}$ miles of navigable river? Is there a simpler and more effective way of doing it?

Pershore Millennium harbour

The overall concept of the importance of appropriate riverside moorings for visiting boats had been contained in several Local Authority 'Local Plans' since the mid-1980s. These concepts had been an expression of hope rather than a call for immediate action. It took a combination of the Trust's need to respond to the call for improved moorings from boating visitors to the river, a Wychavon District Council study of Pershore: 'a Town Enhancement report' in 1994 and the possibility of lottery matched funding to change thoughts into action.

Since the demolition of Pershore Watergate and the deepening of Pershore Lock in 1956 made easy access possible, Pershore Recreation Ground, also called King George's Field, has always been a popular spot for visiting boats. It has a pleasant tree-lined river bank and easy access to the middle of the town. The river bank is seldom without a visiting boat throughout the year, and at peak times can become so crowded that boats may have to moor alongside one another. The 1994 study had suggested a small rectangular river basin for visiting craft, and while not particularly attractive, it was at least a move in the right direction. Various other schemes were also discussed, but something better and more imaginative would be needed if it was to receive public support and meet the criteria laid down for lottery funding by the Millennium Commission. Pershore Town Council was very supportive of the whole principle of the proposal. The initiative would have to come from the Trust. Chairman Dr Hall readily accepted the need for prompt action as submission for a grant had to be made by September 1996.

He sought advice, and Council member David Bezzant suggested an approach to recently retired British Waterways architect Peter White, who had great experience in preparation and submissions of similar projects.

Peter White's scheme changed the rectangular basin design into a visually appealing harbour with a water area planted with natural aquatic vegetation, attractive to wildlife, secure mooring for twenty boats, a small teaching area and general landscaping. Additionally the whole river frontage would be piled to provide an increased length of improved mooring. The proposal better linked the river to the town, and thereby enhanced its tourist attraction.

Thanks to active promotion by Dr Hall the scheme, called Pershore Millennium Harbour, received wide support from the local public, and from Pershore Town Council, Wychavon District Council, and the Environmental Agency, which together with the Trust agreed to provide funding of £235,000 for the total of £470,000 required for the whole project. It was an ambitious scheme.

The scheme was rejected by the Millennium Commission for not having 'as distinctive an impact as others we have received'; their funding grants tended to favour competitive sports rather than recreational projects. While this rejection was a great disappointment to all those involved, the benefit of hindsight enables a more dispassionate view to be taken of the whole project. A landscaped basin with aquatic shore line vegetation, as part of a public recreation area, would need constant upkeep if it was to retain its attractive appearance at all times, and a basin off the line of the main stream could be liable to silt up over a period of years.

However, all was far from lost: the whole river frontage was piled, a concrete walkway laid and mooring posts installed, enhancing both the appearance of the river bank and greatly improving the ease of mooring for boat users. The cost was £127,000, of which the Trust found £10,000. From the Trust's point of view the result was a very positive one.

Evesham Lock

During the 1998-99 winter new steel top gates were fitted at Evesham Lock. While the lock was dewatered the top cill was modified to allow single full length (72ft) narrow boats to pass through the lock. They could fit in the lock chamber before modification, but only with great difficulty. Access to the site was also greatly improved, as was the lockkeeper's access to the far side of the lock, by means of a low level walkway on the new top gates.

The 1998 flood

The second week in April 1998 was a wet one, following on from a fairly wet March. River levels were up, but were still nothing out of the ordinary for the time of year; boats could move with care. But on the night of Wednesday 8 April and all the following day there was very heavy rainfall throughout the Midlands. Many local people have said that they have never experienced such prolonged heavy rain. The ground was waterlogged anyway, and the rain, unable to soak into the ground, flowed down any slope to the lowest level it could find. It was flowing across fields, through hedges, across roads. The ground itself could not be seen, everywhere was covered with a few inches of moving water. Ditches and smaller streams could not cope with the volume of water, nor could the river. There was just nowhere for the water to go.

By midday on Thursday 9 April the river was well over its banks and rising rapidly, and it was still raining. The rate of rise of the river level took everyone by surprise; it was a new experience, like the rate of rainfall, for the Environmental Agency, even for its longer serving ex-National Rivers Authority staff; it was also a new experience for those of us who had lived and worked by and on the river for many years.

Eventually the flood peaked on Good Friday, 10 April, the peak passing Evesham at about noon. It was subsequently found to be the highest flood on record, surpassing the Great Flood of 1900. The rate of rise was also unprecedented.

There were sadly some fatalities along the length of the valley, and many rescues were made of people trapped in low lying caravans, houses and from boats and motor vehicles stuck in the water. A number of bank-side caravan sites were overwhelmed and many scores of so-called mobile homes were swept down the river, being broken up as they hit obstructions like large trees and bridges.

Flood levels dropped relatively quickly over the next two days, leaving behind a vast trail of debris in fields and hedges. Farmers spent many days clearing their fields and hedges and reinstating washed-away fences. Many small and medium sized boats were eventually recovered from fields many miles downstream of their moorings. Others were lost or damaged beyond repair.

Being the Easter Bank Holiday weekend, a number of hire craft were out on the river, which had to be abandoned and the hirers rescued. Some privately-owned boats were also out, including one marooned in Fladbury Lock, from where its crew of two courageous and determined ladies refused to be rescued, even when the occupants of a hire boat alongside them were rescued by helicopter.

Evesham lock house, the lower floor of which was constructed eight inches above the then highest recorded flood level (1900) was cut off, the lower floor submerged to a depth of two feet six inches, which made the level at that site three feet two inches above the previously recorded high level. The lockkeeper and his wife had to be rescued. Being a wooden structure supported on only ten legs, the whole building was potentially vulnerable, particularly if struck by a heavy floating object such as a displaced boat.

The Trust's office at Wyre was also inundated. Fortunately, with most permanent staff working from home, the Trust's current day-to-day records were not affected. Unfortunately most of the old records going back to 1950, minute books, account books, correspondence, and photographic records of most of the works carried out from the mid-1950s right up to 1998 were all destroyed. The absence of much of this irreplaceable source material has caused some problems in checking some of the information in this narrative, and explains the paucity of much pictorial record, especially that since 1970.

Two weeks after the floods the whole length of the Navigation was checked by T.J. Rose, R. Borley and D.C.B. Mathews in *City*. They were able to report a clear navigation channel throughout, but boat crews were advised to proceed with caution as there could have been, and may still be now, various underwater obstructions left by the flood. Volunteer working parties cleared much debris from lock sites.

13 General Matters

Manpower

The role of 'volunteers' in both the restoration and subsequent operation of the Lower Avon Navigation needs to be recorded.

Right from the very start, in 1950, much of the heavy unskilled and semi-skilled work was done by volunteer working parties organised by Barwell: clearing of scrub and other vegetation, manual excavations, silt clearance, painting, making and installation of mooring posts on lock-sides, simple brickwork repairs, simple do-it-yourself joinery and occasional assistance for skilled craftsmen were among the many jobs done. These tasks could not be done by paid labour anyway, because in those early days, there was no money to pay anyone.

Skilled work such as making and installing lock gates, or rebuilding large areas of brickwork was another matter; that had to be paid for, as did large scale works, but only as money was raised could these bigger tasks be done. In any case, it was the Trust's policy that all work should be done to the highest standards and where such standards were unaffordable, the job had to wait until funds were available. Sometimes, when the job could not wait, make-do-and-mend had to be a temporary solution, and volunteer labour was sometimes used for this.

As the Trust started to acquire its work boats, volunteers performed the vital task of moving these vessels on the river. New lock gates were collected from Diglis Workshops at Worcester and equipment taken to isolated sites. Initially the towing was done by the volunteer concerned using his own cruiser. These particular volunteers were 'special' in that they needed both excellent boat handling skills and vessels of appropriate power, and they had to be willing to use their cruisers in this way, which, at times, had its problems. In 1963 the tug *City* was acquired and selected volunteers became tugmasters.

In the early days of the Trust, large scale volunteer working parties would tackle quite large jobs. My early involvement in 1951 was with one of these groups at Fladbury Lock, where we had the task of clearing the area in front of the decayed top gates so that a timber stank could be installed. Large scale working parties took a lot of organising. Volunteer workers were really better suited to small scale tasks, and preferably to those which did not have tight time restraints.

Current working practices are largely governed by Health and Safety requirements, which now inhibit large scale jobs being done by untrained, unskilled, inexperienced people.

Lock restoration work was always done by contractors. Locks at Chadbury★, Fladbury, Wyre, Pershore and later Evesham were restored this way, as was 'the last 600 yards', but preliminary site clearance was normally a task for volunteers, as was tidying up afterwards.

As the work of the Trust expanded over the years, there was a need to employ staff. The Trust's first Secretary, part-time, received only a very modest honorarium and was for

★*The 'contractor' for Chadbury Lock restoration 1952-53 was No.1 ESD Royal Engineers.*

many years the only person to be paid. As work loads increased and more time was required so the honoraria and people involved increased. To recruit staff for various jobs – initially just the Secretary, then lock-keepers, an Assistant Treasurer, a Registration Officer, and later, maintenance staff, the Trust adopted a policy of trying to attract active, recently retired people with a direct interest in waterways matters and relevant experience for the particular job. Their ability and willingness to do the particular job for a very modest honorarium plus specified expenses, and in the case of lock-keepers a rent free house, enabled the Trust to do much of its work on the proverbial shoe-string. The combined experiences of many working lifetimes in many different fields was also of great intangible value; the Trust was very fortunate in this way and owes much to those people.

Members of the Trust Council, its directors in Company Law, are specifically prevented by the Trust's Memorandum and Articles from receiving any payment for their services. Only in more recent years has recognition been given to the fact that some of them come from long distances to do specific work for the Trust, apart from their attendance at routine meetings, and mileage expenses can now be claimed.

Volunteer labour has its disadvantages: normally it is only available at weekends; a specified standard of work is not always possible; it can only be requested and not ordered to do a job; a lot of organisation is necessary to ensure that appropriate equipment and materials are available and that relevant safety precautions are taken.

Employment of paid contractors, on the other hand, takes most of the worry from the job. The employer can require the task to be done how, where and when it wants. It becomes the contractor's responsibility to provide necessary equipment, to obtain materials, to comply with relevant legislation and to deliver what the employer requires. This can be comparatively expensive, but is nearly always more efficient other than for the smallest jobs. It becomes a case of 'horses for courses'.

A regular, organised function of the Trust's volunteers is that of the Reachmaster. Normally two of these are allocated to each lock. It is their joint responsibility to do routine maintenance and inspection of the lock structure, gates and paddle gear and to keep the lock site tidy. Any defects beyond the capability of the Reachmaster to remedy are reported for action by others. The Reachmasters are also responsible for knowing what is happening on the reach above 'their' lock. Unauthorised mooring, a sunken boat, fallen trees and a change of riparian ownership are typical of the observations made and reported for subsequent action by others. Reachmasters are, in effect, the eyes and ears of the Trust on the river.

Another duty undertaken by volunteers is the manning of those locks without resident lockkeepers on Sundays and bank holidays from the Spring Bank Holiday to the end of September. Originally instituted to help the large numbers of inexperienced hire craft users move relatively fast through the locks, the volunteer lock rota has been operated since 1955.

A specific volunteer task is that of Wharfmaster, whose duties are the efficient storage and stock control of materials and equipment, including workboats kept at the Trust's Maintenance Wharf.

The use of unpaid voluntary labour by the Trust has undoubtedly saved the Trust many thousands of pounds over the years, and provides an opportunity for an unusual form of voluntary unpaid service to the community. If such work had to be remunerated, a different system would have to be evolved which would greatly reduce the numbers of people involved. Whether it is now the most efficient system for doing some of the tasks undertaken is open to debate.

Amalgamation with the Upper Avon Navigation Trust

Once the Navigation of the Upper Avon had been restored and reopened in 1974, many people, including members and supporters of both the Upper Avon Navigation Trust (UANT) and the Lower Avon Navigation Trust (LANT), queried the need for two separate organisations to operate what was, and is, a total length of navigable river of just over 45 miles.

The matter was first raised formally at an Extraordinary General Meeting of LANT, called especially for the purpose, in 1975. Subsequent discussions concluded that amalgamation was not in the best interests of LANT at that time.

The Trust had worked closely with UANT since 1971, both through formal discussions and through informal working parties, which discussed matters of mutual interest and concern. Upper Avon tolls were, and are, collected at Evesham Lock.

During the late 1970s, both organisations were fully occupied and committed with their own respective problems. The Navigation of the Upper Avon is to all intents and purposes a new Navigation, with new structures, many of them on new sites, and with newly imposed water retention levels. The Navigation of the Lower Avon is basically a seventeenth century one, designed and built for conditions of that time, which has undergone major restoration in the eighteenth and twentieth centuries, and which retains most of its original size of lock structure and siting, and its inherited water retention levels.

Because the Upper Avon Navigation was 'renewed' rather than 'restored', and the Lower Avon Navigation 'restored' rather than 'renewed' the renewal/restoration processes and the decisions taken about them by each respective Navigation Trust were entirely different, and each evolved and developed along different lines. They were both financially self-sufficient, subject to grants; both did much the same job but in different ways. The main differences were physical, in legal composition and in management; the first two presented no problem to amalgamation; the third would need careful consideration.

In 1984, at the instigation of the supportive Severn Trent Water Authority, further discussions were held, but concluded in 1986 that 'while amalgamation was desirable the time was not yet opportune.'

In 1987 draft identical bye-laws were submitted to the Department of the Environment by UANT and LANT. They were published for public consultation, and were subsequently approved and adopted. The following year the various classifications (sizes and usage) of craft for registration purposes were adjusted and made identical. So gradually some of the differences were removed, and co-operation on matters of direct mutual concern became easier.

Discussions between both parties continued during the late 1980s, and the final *Amalgamation Evaluation Report,* produced in February 1991 by P.H. Ogden, Chairman and J.F. Holroyd, Treasurer, representing the views of UANT and T.W. Gray, Chairman, and D.C.B. Mathews, Council Member representing LANT, observed that it was hard to put forward a sound case for amalgamation in the short term, but it generally favoured amalgamation as a long term measure and invited both Councils to give the amalgamation option serious consideration. The report also noted that the Committee had evaluated the difficulties of amalgamation and concluded that none of these should preclude the merger option, but that there were differences between the two Trusts which would have to be resolved if amalgamation were to proceed.

The Councils of both Trusts held special meetings, separately, to consider the *Amalgamation Evaluation Report* in November 1991. At both meetings objections were raised to amalgamation, which appeared not to have been addressed in the report. However, both Councils accepted that if the many reservations and difficulties could be resolved to the satisfaction of all concerned then, axiomatically, there could no longer be any objection to amalgamation; but it was further recognised that general support for amalgamation would need not only the resolution of all the objections, but also the identification of positive benefits. Thus both Councils agreed independently that, subject to the resolution of all the reservations, the two Trusts should amalgamate within two to five years. Independently they set up their own amalgamation sub-committees to examine in detail and report on the implications of amalgamation: T.W. Gray, D.C.B. Mathews and R. Ward for LANT and Dr D.N.F. Hall, K.R. Ball and R. Cresswell, for UANT.

Following the UANT Annual General Meeting in May 1992, when four new members, who opposed the amalgamation discussions, were elected to their Council, an invitation was offered to any of the new members to join the UANT amalgamation sub-committee. This invitation was taken up in November but the member then resigned in January 1993.

The sub-committees met, independently, a number of times, and jointly on eight occasions under the chairmanship of Dr Hall. On those occasions Mrs P. Edwards, the Secretary of LANT, acted as Secretary to the combined sub-committees.

A final report *LANT/UANT Amalgamation – The Balance of Interests* was published in March 1993 (dated February). The report was detailed and set out very clearly how, both practically and in legal terms, amalgamation could be achieved. It recommended an immediate start to the processes required (set out in the report) to achieve formal amalgamation. In April 1993 LANT Council accepted the report in principle. UANT Council, however, did not accept the report and resolved not to discuss the matter for ten years. Approaches to UANT in 1994 provoked the answer 'there is no useful purpose to be served by reopening the negotiations.'

And there for the moment the matter rests. It takes two to tango!

The Avon Weirs Trust

Weirs on the Avon were originally built as part of the impounding structures for the various water mills (unlike weirs on the Severn downstream from Stourport which were constructed solely for navigation purposes), and all of them pre-date by many years – in some cases by several centuries – the construction of navigation works by William Sandys in the seventeenth century.

While the mills continued to operate, as most of them did until the late nineteenth or early twentieth century, the ownership of the weirs and responsibility for their upkeep was that of the miller. Failure to keep the structures in proper repair would severely endanger the millers' source of water power; and so they were all generally well maintained.

With the cessation of water-powered mill operations during the twentieth century, there was less incentive to maintain the weirs to high standards, although most owners of mill property took their long-established legal right to their head of water very seriously. Alternative uses: operation of turbines, efficient trapping of eels, electricity generation, all required a head of water. The basic form of these old weir structures is described at the beginning of this narrative.

When the Lower Avon Navigation Trust was formed in 1950, the Trust acquired only seven locks and two watergates. Apart from the spill weirs in the two watergate structures, all other weirs on the Lower Avon were in private or corporate ownership. Wyre Mill Productions Ltd, bought by Barwell and colleagues in 1953, had two weirs at Wyre; when Wyre Mill Club was set up in 1954 title of the weirs passed to the Trust. Evesham Weir, with lock and adjoining land, was given to the Trust in 1957. Pershore Weir and Chadbury Weir were bought by the Trust for nominal sums in 1962 and 1971 respectively. No one would admit to responsibility for upkeep of Nafford Weir, so when it needed essential repairs from time to time the Trust stepped in. Berwick Brook Weir was small and of little significance, and had been rebuilt by the Severn Trent Water Authority (STWA) in 1971.

Continued responsibility for these structures was a worry to the Trust. The cost of their upkeep was a very significant part of the cost of maintaining the Navigation as a whole, and in some years greatly exceeded the expenditure on lock structures.

Back in the 1970s, as related elsewhere in this story, the Trust had established useful working relationships with Local Authorities and other outside bodies. Inspection trips and informal meetings were held as and when there were matters of mutual interest to see or discuss. When the STWA succeeded the Severn River Board in 1974, the Trust ensured that the Chairman and Vice-Chairman and principal officers of their Regional Land Drainage Committee (RLDC) were taken on a detailed inspection trip of the river, and a good rapport was established. The STWA RLDC formed a River Avon Steering Group (RASG), with members from the Trust, its Upper Avon neighbour and riparian District Councils. This Group met on an ad hoc basis; depending on the matters discussed the composition of the Group varied. The STWA was later 'privatised' and became Severn Trent Water (STW). The degree of co-operation is well demonstrated by the prompt support of the STW RLDC during the 1987 Wyre Weir crisis recounted elsewhere.

Following the near disaster at Wyre in 1987, the RASG suggested to the STW RLDC that the condition of all the old weir structures on the whole of the Avon between Tewkesbury and Stratford-Upon-Avon should be properly investigated by professional consulting engineers to define the scope of the problem, assess the remaining life of the structures, and estimate the cost of further studies and the cost of necessary remedial work. The investigation was to cover seven weirs on the Lower Avon and two on the Upper Avon. By the time they produced a comprehensive report in 1989 the National Rivers Authority (NRA) had taken over the land drainage and flood control functions of STW.

The report revealed no surprises, but it confirmed that most of the structures were in a poor state of repair – they had been patched and patched again over the years – and were in need of urgent and full scale attention. Failure of any of the control structures on the river, including weirs, dams, sluices and to a lesser extent locks, would affect water levels along the length of the river, with serious implications for drainage, amenity uses and tourism as well as for navigation. Consequential changes in river flow could also damage flood defences, wharfs, moorings, walls and river banks by undercutting and slippage. Few

Work on Chadbury Weir bythe Avon Weirs Trust, 1997.

of the structures were owned by NRA; LANT owned four, some were owned by UANT, others were owned privately and of some the ownership was unknown.

The preliminary estimate of total costs for repairs was put at well in excess of £800,000; this large sum would have to be raised from and by all the parties with an interest in the continued existence of the structures. While taking a leading role in discussions, the NRA felt it was inappropriate for them to take the lead in fund-raising, as the benefits of restoring the structures would be much wider than just for flood control.

The principle parties concerned with the successful outcome of the project were the NRA, LANT, UANT, Tewkesbury Borough Council, Wychavon District Council, and Stratford District Council. Accordingly they agreed to form a charitable trust, the Avon Weirs Trust (AWT) with four trustees, one appointed by the NRA, one by the two Navigation Trusts, one by the three Local Authorities and one to represent the private owners. T.W. Gray, then Chairman of LANT Council, was the nominated trustee of the Navigation Trusts; on his retirement as LANT chairman, he became chairman of the AWT trustees. In August 1991, a programme of work based on the consulting engineers' report was approved, with NRA, later succeeded by the new Environmental Agency (EA), acting as project manager.

The early 1990s were a period of general economic recession, but the AWT was successful in raising funds from a number of sources, the largest contributions coming from Local Authorities and from LANT, which provided £5,000 per year for five years. The Fisheries, Recreation and Conservation department of the NRA provided £30,000 towards the environmental aspects of the works, and there were many donations from private individuals. The various schemes were eligible for grants from the Ministry of Agriculture, Fisheries and Food (MAFF). An abortive attempt was made by the AWT to

Work on Fladbury Weir by Avon Weirs Trust 1997.

obtain money from the Heritage Lottery Fund, but the process of applying proved so bureaucratic that the reconstruction works were completed before a decision had been made by the Fund. It was not possible to receive monies retrospectively.

Work on the nine weirs involved was done in four phases, corresponding with the urgency for completion, starting in 1993 and completed in 1997. To ensure the future maintenance and repair of the nine weirs the EA agreed to undertake the full responsibility for their upkeep. To enable them to do this, it was necessary to transfer the ownership and management to the EA and its successors. The four LANT weirs at Pershore, Wyre (2 weirs), Chadbury and Evesham are now leased to the EA and its successors on a 999 year lease. Ownership of the remaining weirs has passed to the EA.

The total cost of the works was in excess of £2 million, which was very considerably more than the first estimates. The overall extent of the works was greater than the first survey had shown and inflation also increased costs. Encouraged by the success of the AWT, which raised over £220,000, and by the wide interest shown by outside sources, the NRA/EA, helped by large grants from MAFF, made the major contribution towards the overall costs of the whole project.

Its work having been completed by doing the refurbishment and by the vesting of control of the structures in the hands of the EA, the AWT was wound up in 1999.

LANT benefited greatly from the whole project; for a comparatively modest financial contribution, it had transferred future liability for four structures to a responsible National Agency.

Epilogue

The conclusion to a history of the Lower Avon Navigation Trust must inevitably speculate on some of the might-have-beens of the last fifty years.

If the Inland Waterways Association had not come forward when it did, and if Barwell had not taken his boat holiday in 1949, it is almost certain that the river would have rapidly fallen into complete dereliction. This dereliction might well have continued for several decades, pleasure steamers and tripping launches continuing to operate within their 'ponds'. Possibly only now in the current climate of restoration would something be done. How many other restoration schemes of the 1960s and 1970s would have started when they did, had it not been for the pioneering success of the Lower Avon restoration?

Had the restoration started in, say, the 1980s or later, on what would have been a completely derelict navigation, how would the problems have differed? Probably the state of most of the locks and weirs would have brought about a situation similar to that of the Upper Avon in the late 1960s and early 1970s: locks needing completely new structures and some on different sites; perhaps new and different retention levels on some reaches to be negotiated and established; much would depend on whether the legal title to the Navigation had been abandoned. On top of all this would be concerns for conservation and disturbance of habitats; heritage interests would undoubtedly want the old watergates preserved. Health and Safety, Environmental and Planning legislation would all require a different approach.

Initially there would be the same need, as in 1950, to establish public support and credibility for a restoration scheme. With the hurdle of general public support surmounted, there would be an urgent need to negotiate with local Planning Authorities, the Environment Agency (on land drainage issues), conservationists, environmentalists and industrial archeologists regarding treatment of various sites and structures. Having secured agreement in principle from all these diverse groups, from where would the vast amount of money needed come and how would it be raised? There is more public funding available from various sources now than in the 1950s, when there was none; nevertheless stringent conditions would have to be met. It would probably all be just as mind stretching, but in different ways!

A significant social achievement of the Lower Avon restoration was the harmony established, at least within the Trust, of different social groups working together for a common cause. In the early 1950s social differences and boundaries were more clearly defined than now. Some insular attitudes, including my own Vale of Evesham ones, changed towards the 'Brummies' when we found that together we had the challenge of doing with others something that had not been done before.

In a wider field, a clear demonstration was given to the community, both local, regional and national, that self-help groups, if properly led, could achieve worthwhile objectives. Nearer home, the Trust showed that the very beautiful Avon valley could be conserved and used without detriment to the landscape or to its wildlife.

The key to it all, as with most projects, was the clear vision, agreed and accepted by all involved, of what should be the ultimate goal. Having established a tangible objective, it follows that there must be clear and decisive leadership. That leadership will select the right workforce team to carry the project forward at all levels, and will ensure that all the varied tasks are done as and when needed. Leadership will also generate enthusiasm and dedication for the tasks.

The local and regional communities and boat users are fortunate that all the right things happened, and the right people came along as and when they did.

A conclusion to a narrative such as this should try to look forward too. What next for the Trust? Perhaps a better question might be: what next for the navigation of the Lower Avon?

Over the past three hundred or so years, the Navigation has seen times of prosperity and times of decline. Recent river usage peaked about twenty years ago, since when there has been a gradual but perceptible decrease in numbers of registered vessels. It is too early to say if this is an indication for the future.

Earlier in this story, in 1974 and again in 1979, the Trust had taken a look at itself and at the way it worked. Comment is made about the current relevance of the questions then posed. In the 1990s the Way Forward Group addressed in detail the working practices of the Trust; they did not address the medium or long term future.

The present operation of the navigation of the Lower Avon is basically repetitive routine: similar problems recur – from lock maintenance and repairs, to revenue collection and general administration. It is hard, mostly routine work, involving in all a considerable number of people; – and all for only eight locks and twenty-eight miles of navigable river. Many of those people are so involved with day-to-day matters that they have no time to look to the longer-term future.

Thirty or forty years ago, even active business people were so able to organise their time that they could find a sufficient and often a quite considerable amount of time to be closely involved in the direction of the Trust. Today, working pressures for most people just do not allow them to spend that amount of time on Trust business. Their role therefore has to be different, and administrators are employed to ensure that the routine work of the Trust runs efficiently.

The main task of the Trust Council members should be to take a long-term strategic view and consider how the objectives laid down in the Mission Statement and in its Memorandum can best be carried forward for the next fifty years. Many, if not all of them, will not be actively around in ten or fifteen years time, and a firm base for the future must be established now.

Amalgamation with UANT may be part of the answer, but that is certainly only a very small step forward; more will be needed.

Having restored and established a well-maintained navigation, should the Trust be looking for another and larger authority to take over its management, while turning itself into a mandatory consultative body? Would a private limited company, with a small board of directors be a more efficient way to run the navigation, possibly backed by a charitable support/consultative group?

There are several options open; one that seems not viable is that of retaining for much longer the existing methods of direction and management.

The Trust's principle object is 'To maintain and improve the Navigation…' If a forward thinking organisation, on its own, or as part of a larger group, can follow this object and build on the foundations laid by The Lower Avon Navigation Trust over the last fifty years, the future of the Navigation can be assured.

Appendices

APPENDIX A: Nash's History of Worcestershire, 1781, Page 446, under 'Fladbury'

'The work on the River Avon was begun in the year 1635, by Mr William Sandys, son of Sir William Sandys, of Miserden in the County of Gloucester… Evesham, the principal town, importeth the name to the vale through which runneth the Avon, the subject of this work, which river, arising in Northamptonshire, runneth through Warwickshire and so into Gloucestershire, and increasing with other streams that fall into it. To omit places of lesser note, it passeth by Warwick, Stratford, Bidford, Evesham, Pershore, and near Tewkesbury dischargeth itself into the Severn. This Avon never bore boat of any burden before industrious Mr Sandys, beginning his unexpected work in March, 1635, in three years made it possible for vessels to carry forty or fifty tons from the mouth thereof, where it entereth the Severn at Tewkesbury, to Stratford, being about twenty-four miles by land, but nearly fifty by water, through foul and shallow bottoms, and especially through the deep vale of Evesham, purchasing with excessive charge mills, meadow ground, and other lands, cutting in some places a course through the fine land for this waterwork, besides the old main channel, and for the accomplishing hereof he both made sluices at Tewkesbury, in the County of Gloucester, Strensham, Nafford, Pershore, Piddle, Fladbury, Chadbury, Evesham, Harringham, Clive Prior, all in the County of Worcester, Bidford, in the County of Warwick, Welford in the County of Gloucester, and Stratford in the County of Warwick, and so wrought two sluices, keeping up the water that in the summer time vessels of great burden go to Stratford, when others, for lack of water in the Severn, cannot reach Worcester. He erected also wears in the quickest streams, nor did Mr Sandys intend to finish his work at Stratford, but had thoughts to extend the same to Warwick, but what hindered his design, I know not, and for the expense he had heretofore bestowed, it cannot be reckoned less than twenty thousand pounds. The benefits which arose to this county by this extraordinary performance were very many, but I will only add this one, that the Vale of Evesham heretofore laboured under extreme want of firing, and so was forced in these exceeding foul ways to fetch coals from far remote places, but now, by Mr Sandys' industry and labour, it is so contrived that many of them have their coals delivered at their doors. Having so nearly completed this great work and, as some say, spent all his fortune, he immediately delivered up all to the Parliament, to do what more they thought fit. And this much to the honour of worthy Mr Sandys.'

APPENDIX B: *From the* History of Evesham *by George May 1834*

'But although this gentleman [Mr Sandys] only *partially* completed the navigation to Evesham (as will hereafter be proved; notwithstanding the account inserted in Nash, and thence repeatedly copied), he had so far succeeded, as to have obtained from Charles I letters patent…

During the protectorate, [1647-60] William Say, esq. (subsequently one of the judges appointed for the trial of the king, and one whose signature appears upon the warrant for his execution) undertook to complete what Mr Sandys had left unfinished. Purchasing from the owners of the land, (to avoid dispute), liberty to erect sluices, with the necessary embankments, and to make channels: by which means he *completed* the navigation between Tewkesbury and Evesham; which his predecessor had, to a certain extent, executed.

Upon the restoration of Charles the Second [1660], Mr. Say was attainted. Whereupon all his possessions, including his property in this river, became forfeited to the king: who granted the same to trustees…from whom, Thomas lord Windsor purchased the same in 1664.

In the 14th of Charles II. An act passed for making navigable the Stower and Salwarp…in which was contained a clause, that the rivers already made navigable by Mr Sandys, (Mr Say's name being studiously omitted), should be preserved; and that all differences, respecting making further navigation, should be adjusted by commissioners, named therein. In virtue of this clause, lord Windsor, by articles dated 7th November, 1664, agreed with Andrew Yarrenton, Richard Turton, Richard Bartlett and Nicholas Baker, that they, at their own cost, should, on or before the 8th of September, 1666, make this river navigable from Evesham to the town of Stratford. Which they accordingly did: erecting six sluices, with their accompanying embankments thereupon. Completing, with those originally constructed by Mr. Sandys and Mr. Say, a total of fourteen locks and 'aires' between Stratford and the Severn.

By the above completion of Mr. Sandy's spirited enterprise, throughout a course of fifty miles, this town and vale are abundantly supplied with coals; and water communication is further effected, by aid of the Severn and canals, with every part of the kingdom.'

Footnote (by May) to the above: 'It may be here remarked, that the first attempt toward propelling vessels by steam-power, was made upon the Avon, at Evesham, by Jonathan Hulls, of Campden: who, in December, 1736, obtained a patent for his invention; and in the following year published a description of his steam-boat; copies of which are now become extremely rare. The title of that publication is "A description and draught of a new-invented machine, for carrying vessels or ships out of or into any harbour, port or river, against wind and tide, or in a calm." By Jonathan Hulls. London: 1737 – Vide Edinburgh Philosophical Journal, vol. ix.p.274.'

APPENDIX C: *The last almost through journey – 1938*

In the first volume of his autobiography *Landscape with Machines* L.T.C. Rolt, the author of *Narrow Boat*, gives a brief account of a holiday on the river in 1938.

He travelled from Wyre Piddle in a converted ship's lifeboat *Miranda* upstream through, and operating, Cropthorne Watergate to the tail of Chadbury Lock, which at the time was 'stopped' for repairs to the leaking gates. He turned downstream to Tewkesbury and on to the Severn.

He returned to Wyre Piddle, getting stuck on a shoal in the middle of Wyre Lock on the way. This may well have been the last through journey, or in this case the last almost through journey, made before that part of the river upstream from Pershore became derelict.

APPENDIX D: *A consulting engineer at Chadbury Lock – Correspondence between D.H. Burlingham and C.D. Barwell.*

From D.H. Burlingham to C.D. Barwell, 6 May 1952

Since speaking to you on the telephone on Friday I have thought more about what you told me, especially about the Consultant Engineer, and although I know you are very busy at the present time I feel I must put my thoughts on the matter in writing.

I do not know the circumstances which commit you to employ Cyril Boucher & Partners, but I do feel that Chadbury Lock Sub-Committee should have been told about this at the beginning. In fact I do not see now the usefulness of this Committee as we can make no decisions – in fact our work will be done by the Consultant Engineers.

I do feel that the people we have on our Committee, – in particular Messrs Bomford, Madge & Tuckwood – are perfectly capable of deciding (with your guidance) what should be done and how, and of supervising all work if necessary. All of them are, or have been, responsible persons used to such work and it is doubting their capabilities, having an outside Engineer. If we feel we want advice, we can always ask for it.

There is of course the expense of employing C.B. & P. This is a bit out of my province but it must be at least the monetary value of several loads of Cement, and money which, from what I understand of the Trust's finances, we can ill afford.

Another angle is that the Evesham 'Save the Avon' organization (sic) is going to have a hard enough task to raise money for what is actually done, let alone for paid supervision etc.

I feel that local firms will be able to do all the necessary work and will be pleased to do it – for payment of course. I am told that it should be possible to do the whole Restoration for about £3,000, and do it really well. Certainly it should be possible to rebuild all the walls round the gates and to lay new concrete platforms round both sills for about £1,000.

I feel that we must either, as a Committee, work out our Salvation or cease as a Committee, as we should be unable to serve any useful purpose.

You may not agree with the views already expressed, but I do feel that as Chadbury is an Evesham affair the decisions of what is to be done and how should be left to those who have now been asked to make such decisions. I would therefore suggest that if it is at all possible Messrs C.B. & P's services be dispensed with.

The above remarks are written and intended in a friendly spirit, but at the moment I do feel rather strongly on this most vital matter, and I should be glad to know exactly what the position is well before the Meeting on Monday. If our Committee continues, once we have got going, you can rely entirely on our getting the work done and done properly without any worry to yourself.

From C.D. Barwell to D.H. Burlingham, 7 May 1952

In regard to our Consulting Engineers Messrs Cyril Boucher and Partners, I hasten to reassure you on this matter and say to you, do not concern yourself about their connection with this work. We will discuss this more fully on Monday, but in the meantime, in view of your comments and the fact that you have mentioned this to several of your Committee Members, I feel it adviseable (sic) to now give you the full story behind this situation, which I may add is not to my making nor to my liking.

Here then is the story; some five years ago the IWA. was formed in London by Robert Aickmann, Peter Scott, Sir A.P. Herbert and others, in an attempt to prevent a large number of Waterways in this Country from becoming derelict and lost for ever. They appointed C.B. & P. as their Hon. Consultants with the agreement that if at any time major work was undertaken by IWA on any of these Waterways that C.B. & P. would be appointed Official Consultants at the usual fees. In 1949, before I had become a member of the Midlands Branch of IWA or even thought of purchasing the Avon, the Midlands Branch had been considering the possibility of doing something with the Avon Navigation. There were two reasons for this, the first, that several members of the Committee were owners of Cruisers and desired to travel to Pershore and if possible to Evesham, the second, that the Evesham Borough were already very concerned about the state of the Evesham Pound and a proposal had been made by Mr Huxley that Chadbury Lock be replaced by a dam. As a result of this statement made in the Evesham Journal, the Chairman of IWA wrote a strong reply and the result was that the Midlands Branch took a direct interest in the Avon. I happened to come along at the same time, full of fury because I could not get my craft to Pershore, and eventually joined up with the IWA Midlands Branch and purchased the Navigation myself.

During these preliminaries and before my association with the Midlands Branch, Mr Boucher had again been called in by the Local Branch to assist in their deliberations. He had in fact toured all locks between Evesham and Tewkesbury and had prepared a detailed statement reporting fully on the condition of all Locks, Weirs, Sluices, etc and of the general condition of the Reaches between each Lock. For this he made no charge, but the same inference in relation to work done in the future was, I understand, implied. However, when I purchased the Navigation there was nothing in the deeds to show that I was forced to employ C.B. & P. as my Consultants, and in fact, I acted on my own behalf in this matter when work has been undertaken on the Navigation from the inception of my control and up to the present time.

Chadbury Lock however is rather a different matter; firstly, because Boucher was requested to make a special survey of this Lock in view of Evesham fears in regard to its future – this also was undertaken on an Honorary basis. Secondly, soon after the Trust had been formed Aickmann (a Council Member) agreed to approach Lord Kilmaine of the Pilgrim Trust, and they having met together it was agreed to state a case to go before the Trustees of Pilgrims. Kilmaine however stipulated….

a. That any grant given be for one specific purpose and suggested that Chadbury Lock be the individual item for this purpose

b. That an impartial Consulting Engineer be employed by our Trust to prepare a detailed plan and specification of the work required at Chadbury and the cost thereof.

Boucher therefore had to be called upon to do this work and as we could not give him any guarantee that we would proceed with the repairs, he suggested that he receive a fee of 100-gns for the work which he had already done and which he was now required to do for the purpose of submitting the appeal to the Pilgrim Trust. Naturally I could not see my way to agree this fee, although on making enquiries elsewhere I found that other Consulting Engineers were asking even higher sums for the same services.

Accordingly, I was rather forced to strike a bargain with Boucher, which was that we would meet his out of pocket expenses to date and for the work which he would have to do, providing always that if we undertook major repairs to Chadbury, his Firm would be employed as Official Consultants.

I do not now propose to go further into this matter with you in this letter, but I have my own ideas for the future for circumnavigating a position which I have never sought, and for which I have no need. The employment of the Army at Chadbury, and the establishment of a Works Sub-Committee at Evesham to deal with Chadbury are but two of my ideas for overcoming the problem, and I prefer to say no more now until we meet in private next Monday, when I can explain the steps for the future.

Note: Appendix F 'Consultant £36-15-0', shows that very modest expenses and no fees were claimed. Mr Boucher made several visits to site, but was not directly involved with the work.

APPENDIX E: *Purchasing power of the pound (Bank of England Retail Price Index)*
This appendix is included to help convert earlier costs incurred into 1993 values.

Year	Value	Year	Value	Year	Value
1950	£13.70	1968	£7.18	1986	£1.42
1951	13.19	1969	6.78	1987	1.38
1952	11.70	1970	6.47	1988	1.34
1953	11.22	1971	5.99	1989	1.27
1954	11.08	1972	5.55	1990	1.18
1955	10.65	1973	5.17	1991	1.08
1956	10.13	1974	4.65	1992	1.02
1957	9.73	1975	3.95	1993	1.00
1958	9.39	1976	3.23		
1959	9.21	1977	2.81		
1960	9.24	1978	2.58		
1961	9.06	1979	2.38		
1962	8.67	1980	2.06		
1963	8.45	1981	1.85		
1964	8.29	1982	1.68		
1965	7.94	1983	1.61		
1966	7.62	1984	1.55		
1967	7.36	1985	1.49		

These figures were published in 1994, and give a rough guide to the change in value of the Pound since 1950. A more accurate guide might be obtained by using a Construction Industry Price Index.

APPENDIX F

Chadbury Lock

Analysis of Cost of Restoration Work 1952 & 1953

Gates and Sills	£	s	d
Top Gates Materials	196	10	00
Labour (incl D & IWE Charge)	166	18	08
Bottom Gates Materials	246	19	10
Labour (incl 4 balance arms etc)	234	12	03
	845	00	09

Aggregate			
Gravel 365 tons 10 cwt	276	13	01
Sand 297 tons 3 cwt	175	02	09
662 tons 13 cwt	451	15	10

Cement			
97 tons 8 cwt	423	19	06

Steel 18 tons 7 cwt	807	01	01

Timber (shuttering etc)	328	13	02

Subsistences			
'Chequers'	760	00	00
Miscellaneous	43	12	07
	803	12	07

Spares and Repairs	36	12	05

Land Restoration	78	08	03

Miscellaneous			
Consultant	36	15	00
Charge for use of Trust's Piles	35	12	06
Piling left 'in situ'	54	06	08
Notice Board, Plate, Chains	24	17	01
Transport	15	10	00
Miscellaneous	51	00	04
	218	01	07

TOTAL	£3,993	05	02

APPENDIX G

Wyre Lock

Analysis of Cost of Restoration Work 1954

Repairs to Lock Chamber	£	s	d
Including piling and removal			
of mud, excluding Gate, Cill			
& Quoin repairs	2,755	05	03

Repairs to Gates, Cills and Lock Floors
Including making and fitting
new Downstream Gates

Materials	320	17	06
Labour (incl. gratuities)	322	02	09
	653	00	03

Transport of Gates	19	16	03

Subsistences	4	07	03

Removal of Shoal	50	00	00

Work for Wyre Mill Productions Ltd
Repairs to Weirs, making wall
and filling scour channels,
tree felling and materials

for flood gates	302	16	04

TOTAL	£3,785	05	04

Using the RPI Index (Appendix E) the 1993 equivalent values would be:

£3,993 = £45,759
£3,785 = £41,937

APPENDIX H: *Chadbury Sluice 1971.*

Chadbury sluice was largely reconstructed in June 1971. The structure comprised six wooden vertical lift gates, each of which could be raised on a crude ratchet system operated with a long steel bar. These gates were held in place by seven substantial vertical wooden posts. The stone walls and stone slab floor of the sluice were sound. Part of the sluice had been in fairly recent use as an eel trap. The posts and gates had to be replaced.

The main problem was site access for plant of sufficient size to pile off the area in order to dewater it. An alternative method had to be devised. Falsework consisting of a strong steel fame was made with seven strong arms, each of which could be removed independently from the frame, which also had short feet to hold it about eighteen inches above floor level.

This frame was lowered into the water immediately above the sluice gates, each of its removable arms positioned against one of the vertical posts. The back of the steel frame provided a strong horizontal beam right across the sluice entrance about eighteen inches above the floor and about eight feet from the sluice itself. At the top of the stone walls, almost above the back of the frame, a steel beam was placed horizontally across the sluice and well secured. There were now two strong horizontal beams across the sluice entrance, against which steel piles could be placed without the necessity of having to drive them through the sluice floor. Large tarpaulin sheets (this was before the days of large plastic sheeting) were sunk against the steel piles to make a water seal. This temporary structure enabled the area to be satisfactorily dewatered, and while it did leak, the water level at the lower side of the sluice was such that the whole work area was covered by only about six inches of water, which was acceptable if not ideal.

To remove and replace each vertical wooden post, one steel arm was removed from the frame, the remaining steel arms providing the horizontal support. As each vertical post was renewed, the steel arm was refitted, and the next steel arm removed to access the next wooden post. With all the vertical posts renewed, horizontal support for them was provided by a steel frame bridge across the sluice, to which the vertical posts were fixed and a lower horizontal beam was also provided. The wooden gates were replaced by stiffened quarter inch steel plates with a hole in the top for attaching lifting gear.

It was not envisaged that the sluices would be used very often, and the gate lifting and closing would be done with the digger arm of a JCB tractor.

These small-type sluices were relatively easy to open and notoriously difficult to close. It only needed a very small tree branch, about $\frac{1}{2}$ in thick, to get stuck in the opening to prevent closure. Similar sluice gates existed at Evesham, Fladbury (not owned by the Trust), and Wyre; those previously existing further downstream had been replaced by the Severn Catchment – later River Board, when installing its large gates.

At the end of the job the new sluices were used to dry off Chadbury Weir for inspection. Its condition was generally good and those minor repairs required were done. The contractor for the job was P. Williams and Sons of Defford.

A detailed description of this comparatively small job is given because the solution to the problem was somewhat unorthodox. Peter Williams liked a job, small or large, with a challenge, and the Trust had plenty of those to offer. He and I devised and refined the Chadbury sluice solution until we were satisfied that it could work safely and at a cost acceptable to the Trust. It was the first of many jobs for the Trust, done by P. Williams and Sons. Peter has now retired, but his sons, Mark and Simon, have their father's flair for the unusual.

APPENDIX I: *Lower Avon Navigation Trust Work Boats*

City

A Bantam, 'Pusher' tug, used for commercial and navigation maintenance, 23ft long, 8ft 6in beam and draws 4ft and is powered by a Lister JP3. Built around 1950 by E.C. Jones & Sons of Brentford, she was used at Brentford Docks until 1963, when declared 'surplus to requirements' by BWB. She was then purchased by a small consortium of generous LANT members for use in the maintenance of the Lower Avon. Subsequently, all 'shares' in the vessel were transferred to the Trust by gifts.

Avon Jubilant

A powered general-purpose workboat with a cabin, 25ft long, 8ft beam and draws 9in unladen and is powered by a Lister SR2. Built in 1969 by Seaborne Yacht Co. of Kempsey, Worcester, on the instructions of Douglas Barwell, at his own expense, she was named in celebration of his OBE award. Ownership was later transferred to the Trust.

Lantern

An ex-River Great Ouse, sugar beet barge of 35 tons capacity, 54ft long, 12ft beam, unladen draught 6in. Built in 1939 by an unknown builder and purchased in 1961 by LANT from the British Sugar Corporation. After purchase she was fitted with a ramp and strengthened hold platform for the transport of heavy plant, as well as being used as a dumb barge pushed by *City*. She has now been fitted with an hydraulic SKB Kraner arm, powered by a 2.5 BMC diesel engine, making her a versatile lifting or dredging vessel with capacities varying from 9000 to 2000lbs, the maximum extension being 20ft 4in.

Robert Aickman

A welded steel dumb hopper barge, 40ft length 10ft beam and unladen draught 9in with removable 20 ton capacity hold. Built in 1982 by Watercraft of Evesham and named after the founder and inspirational leader of IWA and founder Council member of LANT.

Douglas Barwell

A second welded steel dumb hopper barge, 40ft length, 10ft beam and unladen draught 9in with removable 20 ton capacity hold. Built in 1991 by Watercraft, who had by then moved to Worcester. Named after the founder and first Chairman of LANT.

Gallant

An aluminium ex-Royal Engineers swim-ended decked bridging pontoon, 17ft 6in long, 5ft 9in wide with a 6in draught, purchased in June 1978 from J.T. Leavesley (Alrewas) Ltd. Originally named *Avon Gallant* but *Avon* now dropped.

Note: *Jubilant, Gallant* and *Lantern* incorporate LANT in the name!

APPENDIX J: *Officers of The Lower Avon Navigation Trust*

Chairmen			*Treasurers*		
1950 – 1969	C.D. Barwell		1950 – 1959	P.H. Protheroe ★	
1970 – 1971	H.S. Goodby		1960 – 1967	W.F. Tunna ★	
1972 – 1978	D.H. Burlingham		1968 – 1971	A.B. Martin ★	
1979 – 1983	D.J. Smith		1972 – 1982	R.J. Turner ★	
1984 – 1989	D.H. Stokes		1983	D.H. Stokes	
1990 – 1993	T.W. Gray		1984 – 1985	G.T. Shepherd	
1994 – 1999	D.N.F. Hall		1986 – 1987	J.J. Tysoe	
1999 –	T.W. Gray		1988 – 1993	R. Edwards	
Secretaries			1994 –	R.J. Harrison	
1950 – 1960	E.J. Price				
1961 – 1964	R.W. Antice				
1965 – 1983	I.M. Beard MBE		★Also managers of Evesham Branch National Provincial/National Westminster Bank.		
1984 – 1988	I.C.J. Morgan				
1989 –	Mrs. P. Edwards				